Ideas of Order
in the Novels
of Thomas Pynchon

MOLLY HITE

OHIO STATE UNIVERSITY PRESS: COLUMBUS

All excerpts from *Gravity's Rainbow*, by Thomas Pynchon, are copyright © 1973 by Thomas Pynchon. Reprinted by permission of Viking Penguin, Inc., 625 Madison Avenue, New York, New York 10022; Jonathan Cape, Ltd., 30 Bedford Square, London WC1, England; and the Melanie Jackson Agency, 1500 Broadway, Suite 2805, New York, New York 10036.

All excerpts from *The Crying of Lot 49*, by Thomas Pynchon, are copyright © 1965, 1966 by Thomas Pynchon. Reprinted by permission of Harper and Row, Publishers, Inc., 10 East Fifty-third Street, New York, New York 10022; Jonathan Cape, Ltd., 30 Bedford Square, London WC1 England; A. M. Heath and Company, Ltd., 40–42 William IV Street, London WC2N 4DD, England; and the Melanie Jackson Agency, 1500 Broadway, Suite 2805, New York, New York 10036.

All excerpts from *V.*, by Thomas Pynchon, are copyright © 1961, 1963, by Thomas Pynchon. Reprinted by permission of Harper and Row, Publishers, Inc., 10 East Fifty-third Street, New York, New York 10022; Jonathan Cape, Ltd., 30 Bedford Square, London WC1 England; A. M. Heath and Company, Ltd., 40–42 William IV Street, London WC2N 4DD, England; and the Melanie Jackson Agency, 1500 Broadway, Suite 2805, New York, New York 10036.

The stanza from "The Idea of Order at Key West," by Wallace Stevens, is from *The Collected Poems of Wallace Stevens*, copyright © 1923, 1931, 1935, 1936, 1937, 1942, 1943, 1944, 1945, 1946, 1947, 1948, 1949, 1950, 1951, 1952, 1954 by Wallace Stevens. All rights reserved under International and Pan-American Copyright Conventions. Reprinted by permission of Alfred A. Knopf, Inc., 201 East Fiftieth Street, New York, New York 10022.

A portion of Chapter 1 has been revised from " 'Holy Center-Approaching' in the Novels of Thomas Pynchon," by Molly Hite, originally published in the *Journal of Narrative Technique*, Vol. XIII, No. 2, pp. 121–29. Reprinted by permission of the publisher.

Library of Congress Cataloguing in Publication Data

Hite, Molly, 1947—
   Ideas of order in the novels of Thomas Pynchon.

   Bibliography: p.
   Includes index.
   1. Pynchon, Thomas—Criticism and interpretation.
2. Order (Philosophy) in literature.   I. Title.
PS3566.Y55Z66   1983   813'.54   83–4258
ISBN 0–8142–0350–7

FOR GERARD H. COX

Contents

Preface

I became interested in Pynchon's work in 1966, when I first read *V*. My immediate reaction to that novel tends to contradict one of the charges most commonly leveled at Pynchon's writing: whether or not Profane, Stencil, and the Whole Sick Crew are "round" or "developed" characters, I was convinced I *knew* them, traveled in some of the same circles, and could recognize the rhythms of their speech in Pynchon's uncannily precise dialogue. A number of my acquaintances shared, and still share, this perception, which extended in due time to *The Crying of Lot 49* and *Gravity's Rainbow*. I was astonished to learn much later that Pynchon is frequently criticized for being the academic's academic, the writer whose books are intended to be taught, not read. For a long time, the most ardent Pynchon fans that I knew were a weight lifter, a short-order cook, and a pizza deliveryman.

Much later, when I was engaged in studying and teaching philosophy, I returned to Pynchon with the vague intention of elevating him to the status of a "philosophical novelist." The conversion process worked in reverse: Pynchon's experiments with narrative conventions made me acutely aware of the fact that every established form of discourse (including the philosophical essay and the philosophical dialogue) has its own embedded assumptions that exert powerful controls over the "subject matter." I drifted slowly from my initial project, a consideration of philosophical concerns in Pynchon's novels, to an increased emphasis on how narrative forms dictate and shape the thematic issues raised in these novels. In the process I drifted over the hazy border between philosophy and literature—and the well-defined border between philosophy departments and English departments. This study is the end product of that long drift.

I am grateful to Charles Altieri and Malcolm Griffith, of the University of Washington English Department, for the attention they gave to the manuscript in its early stages. Both managed, although in very different ways, to wake me from my dogmatic slumbers and make me face questions about literary sense and reference that I might otherwise have passed over. I want especially to thank Richard Dunn, now chairman of that department, who took the time to follow, and guide, this study through all its metamorphoses, and contributed advice and support whenever they were needed, usually on very short notice. Donna Orange, my former colleague in the Seattle University Philosophy Department, asked the right questions and required precise answers: I am grateful for her affection and her integrity. Thanks also are due to Robert Demorest, of the Ohio State University Press, for his thorough and sensitive editing.

I am very grateful to my children, Joshua and Geoffrey, for putting up with me through the writing of this book and for maintaining staunchly that they were proud of my preoccupation. Finally, my most profound thanks go to my husband, Gerard H. Cox, who has been my most demanding reader and severest critic as well as my closest associate. Without his help I doubt that this work could have assumed anything like its present form; he has been an unfailing source of direction and support.

Ithaca, New York
1982

Introduction: Ideas of Order

This book is primarily a study of the novels of Thomas Pynchon, certainly one of the most important fiction writers of the post–World War II period and perhaps the most important. It is also, however, a study of the congeries of ideas designated by the word *order*, and of the implications these ideas have for the shape and substance of narratives. Narratives are orders, or orderly arrangements of signs, of course; and theoretically they can be orders of various kinds, embodying various assumptions about the nature and functions of form, structure, system, connection, relation, accretion, accumulation, unity, coherence, completion, closure, and plot—to suggest just a few of the relations that the demand for, or discovery of, order may imply. Despite the potential for diversity, however, *narrative order* tends to have a quite restricted meaning, to a large extent because narratives have always been tied to dominant social perceptions of reality. The order we demand from, or discern in, stories is related to the order or disorder we understand to be the case in our own lives and worlds: for instance, narrative order may reflect (using its own conventions to set up analogies) what is generally understood to be a just and harmonious universe, or it may stand in ironic opposition to what is generally understood to be a chaotic, antihuman, and inexplicable universe. (That it tends to do one or the other of these two things is to the point.)

Pynchon's narratives are in addition *about* order: about its presence or absence; about order as object of desire, dread, fantasy, or hallucination; about what order means, how it is apprehended, and what it entails. His works thus tend to comment on themselves. His characters look for the hidden structures of their experience that will reveal how events are connected, how everything adds up, what it all means; and these structures reduplicate, oppose, or stand in some other relation to the overall structure of the narrative. Armed with the knowledge that the narrative itself is ordered and that this order is intentional and important, readers enter the quest at a somewhat higher level, but they too are looking for an ultimate pattern or structure, an order that will constitute a reading; and consequently their activity parallels the activities of the characters, with all the possibilities for irony attendant on this situation.

Such devices—self-reference, self-irony, the complex inter-actions and interreactions of questing character and interpret-ing reader—are familiar to most of us from our reading of modernist fiction. But it is in this context that I want to insist on Pynchon's postmodernism. Postmodern fiction tends to attack, undermine, parody, or otherwise call into question certain characteristic assumptions of modernist fiction, just as modernist fiction called into question several of the character-istic assumptions of its precursors, realistic and naturalistic fiction. One persistent quality of Pynchon's work is that it cannot be taken ''straight''; we cannot read it successfully by exercising our knowledge of established conventions, even modernist conventions. In fact, Pynchon seems to go to some lengths to provoke us into applying such conventions, only to confront us with their inadequacy. As Brian McHale has demonstrated recently, Pynchon not only anticipates but encourages a "modernist reading" in order to sabotage contemporary habits of mind that derive from certain of the assumptions of modernism.[1]

These assumptions are not exclusively literary. Modernism was as much a world view as it was an aesthetic, and drew on contemporary developments in the sciences, the social sciences, and philosophy for its defining features. But it also incorporated these features into a largely inherited framework because of its understanding of what order is, of what it means to say that something—a work of art, a cosmos—is ordered or orderly. McHale points out that *Gravity's Rainbow* challenges two expectations we have internalized from literary modernism: that a "real story" lies beneath the frequently convoluted surface of the narrative discourse, and that with some deciphering a stable chronology will be revealed that will naturalize transitions from one character's mind to another's. I would add that in both of these instances Pynchon is flouting conventions that require an explicable coherence from the work of art precisely because the work of art must stand in ironic contrast to the "chaos" of reality. Indeed, it is a central tenet of the modernist ontology that artistic creations are ordered whereas the universe is not. But this tenet depends on a restricted definition of *order*; it admits, finally, only one idea—which becomes The Idea—of order. In all three of his novels to date, Pynchon has parodied this restricted understanding of what order is and implies by taking it to its logical conclusions.

In modernist contexts it often passes as a truism (or a sad-but-truism) that we cannot expect order from the world itself, that apparent order is an imposition of the synthesizing intellect or the harmonizing imagination, that, in the absence of a transcendent God, the source of order can only be the individual human subject. This opinion can be held more or less naïvely, i.e., with a greater or lesser consciousness of what a "chaotic" reality means for human knowledge and desire. It is not held naïvely in the works of Wallace Stevens, who made the dialectic between human imagination and nonhuman reality a central theme throughout his poetic career. For this reason I want to examine briefly a key stanza of his "The Idea of Order at Key West" (1934) as an important expression of the modernist ontology. (I am not advancing an exhaustive reading of the poem, nor do I mean to reduce Stevens's work to the statement of a world view or to pin him to his world view exclusively—after all, "The Idea of Order at Key West" was published in a collection that Stevens entitled *Ideas of Order*.)

In the poem as a whole, the forming and informing of reality is the work of the poetic imagination—"she" in the poem's terms.

> It was her voice that made
> The sky acutest at its vanishing.
> She measured to the hour its solitude.
> She was the single artificer of the world
> In which she sang. And when she sang, the sea,
> Whatever self it had, became the self
> That was her song, for she was the maker. Then we,
> As we beheld her striding there alone,
> Knew that there never was a world for her
> Except the one she sang and, singing, made.

Three characteristics of this idea of order are particularly important for the present discussion. First, the act that bestows order also bestows meaning: "her" song transforms inchoate reality into "world," introducing the theme of transience and loss by making "the sky acutest at its vanishing" and aligning this sky with the human experience of loneliness by "measuring" its duration, an act that transforms singularity into solitude. Order brings significance; that which is not ordered is opaque to the understanding: "Whatever self" the sea had outside "her" song is unknown, but "when she sang, the sea . . . became the self / That was her song, for she was the maker." Second, order is clearly singular here, "*the* world / That was her song" (my emphasis). "She" does not create a number of orders, of which this is one; the order she produces is contingent on her "voice," her act of production, and ceases when she ceases to sing. This leads to the third characteristic: order is something made, an artifact, and thus requires a "maker" or "artificer." It is never simply there; it must come into being, a fact that makes "her" both origin and center of the "world" she creates: "there never was a world for her / Except the one she sang and, singing, made." Order is a human phenomenon in this poem, and because order alone confers significance, we must conclude that reality, apart from the imagination's forming and informing, is meaningless alterity, chaos. Stevens makes this situation the occasion for ironic celebration here: if the poetic imagination is sole author of meaning and order in the world, there is at least a sort of triumph in accepting and acknowledging this state of affairs. In other poems his emphasis falls more poignantly on the lack of fit between the bleak landscape of reality and human aspiration.[2] In either case it is the mind that discerns order and the mind that produces it, a solipsism. "Shall I project a world?" Pynchon's Oedipa Maas asks herself, wondering if *she* can be "the single artificer of the world / In which she sang"; for it seems to her that this is the only way in which "world," or meaningful order, can come into being. But *order* need not mean anything as vast or as subjective as Oedipa's hypothesized "projection."

What is most interesting about the idea of order that I have sketched above is how much it owes to an older theocentric tradition. The notion that seems distinctively modern, that order is subjective and unreal, whereas reality is incomprehensibly disordered, follows logically from a sort of historical sleight-of-hand whereby the theocentric world view lost its God but maintained the rest of its assumptions intact. Paradoxically, all three of the characteristics that I identified above as belonging to the modernist ontology—that order implies meaning; that there is, and can be, only one order, which necessarily encompasses everything that is perceived as ordered; and that order presumes an artificer or maker—are largely traditional, carried over unchanged from a world view that made God the center, origin, and cause of a harmonious and coherent universe. The idea that order implies meaning is still generally accepted; it is a tenet of current information theory, for instance. But the model of order as single and all-encompassing—implying as it does an ultimately unified science of cosmology—and the allied notion that order presumes an orderer are under heavy attack in both philosophical and scientific circles.[3] The argument is simply that neither of these conditions is necessary for there to be order: there can be many orders operating in reality, and different kinds of order; one need not, following the analogy of human artifice, presume that an instance of organization requires an organizer. In the world from which Pynchon borrows some of his most comprehensive metaphors, order is an acknowledged fact and carries no conspiratorial overtones. The overtones come from an older world view and an older discipline, theology.

Within the theocentric tradition, God is often viewed as an artist as well as an artificer, or even an author who plots the course of world history. As long as this God's existence, omnipotence, omniscience, and benevolence are taken for granted, creation can be presumed to be *an* order, in which particular events, however painful and gratuitous they may seem, can be accepted as aspects of an ultimately just divine plan. Something quite quite different happens, however, when the argument is turned around, so that observed order in the physical world becomes *evidence* that an omnipotent, omniscient, and benevolent God exists. In the post-Enlightenment arguments "from design" for the existence of God, we can see the beginnings of a Pynchonesque universe, in which the possibility that someone or something is in charge of The Way Things Are is at least as frightening as the possibility that order is unreal because no one and nothing is in charge of anything.

Such arguments, among the last attempts to establish a scientific basis for religious belief, begin from instances of apparently purposive order in the physical universe—the stately procession of planets around the sun, the intricacies of the human eye—and infer that these complexities cannot be the work of chance and that therefore God exists. The arguments simply presume that occasions of order in the natural world are aspects of a universal order, as yet dimly perceived: thus Sir Isaac Newton reasons, "This most beautiful system of the sun, planets, and comets, could only proceed from the counsel and dominion of an intelligent Being," and rules out the possibility of more than one such being (and more than one such system) by leaping to the conclusion: "This Being governs all things. . . ." Such arguments also presume that God stands in the same relation to creation as a human manufacturer to one of his contrivances: William Paley's popular work *Natural Theology* (1802) explicitly compares the universe to a watch, arguing that if the watch is clearly an artifact, then so is the universe (which after all has many more moving parts).[4]

But as critics of the arguments from design were quick to point out, such reasoning does not justify the conclusion that the maker of a universal order must be *all*-powerful, wise, or (especially) benevolent—in short, what Western culture has traditionally meant by the word *God*. The scientific data on which these arguments are built are at best ethically neutral. On the other hand, the "order" of the world in which human beings live appears increasingly threatening to human existence. In fact, the "order" characterizing the twentieth century seems, ironically, to require an actively malignant artificer, who is bent on bringing history to a quick conclusion.

This line of thought leads directly to Pynchon's fictional worlds. To the question "Who or what is responsible for the order of the universe?" there seem to be two possible answers. The first is: "Some being or beings, perhaps vaguely benign but inept, more probably disinterested or malevolent"—the hypothesis of a V., a Tristero, a Them. The second is: "No one; apparent order is illusory, imposed by our own cognitive functions on a reality that is in itself totally chaotic"—the world view that, as I suggested earlier, is distinctively modernist. Pynchon uses these answers to set up a satiric double bind for his characters. Given this state of affairs, and this question, the only alternative to theology seems to be paranoia.

But the double bind is satiric because it comes from asking the wrong question. "Who or what is responsible" presumes that order is one, not multiple, and that it is the work of some power or being, not simply there. It results from the same kind of thinking that tries to elevate science into cosmology and then sees chaos when science cannot link up its various systems. By confronting his characters with the choice between an outside power imposing order on the world or an *inside* power (either the shaping imagination, or paranoia, or both) imposing order on the world, Pynchon parodies a post-religious attitude that takes these extremes as exhaustive. His own fictional worlds, however, are pluralistic—governed not by a rigid, absolute, and universal Idea of Order but by multiple partial, overlapping, and often conflicting *ideas* of order. And these worlds are familiar, even when they are most bizarre and surreal, because they evoke a multilayered reality in which multiple means of putting things together manage to coexist without resolving into a single, definitive system of organization.

In chapter 1 of this study, "Including Middles," I survey the dichotomy that I have considered above: the propositions that reality is either governed by an externally imposed order or is total chaos; and examine the ways in which Pynchon exploits the tension between these extremes to generate a myth of origins for both freedom and language. The first section of this chapter, " 'Holy-Center-Approaching,' " deals with the hypothesis of a central insight that is unaccountably missing from Pynchon's fictional worlds; I suggest that this absent center functions as a structural trope motivating the radical pluralism of these worlds. In the second section, "Absence, Language, and Freedom," I develop the idea of a pluralistically conceived universe and sketch some of the implications of such a universe for each of the three novels.

Chapter 2, "Duplicity and Duplication in *V*.," takes issue with readings that make *V*. a puzzle novel that can be reassembled to yield an underlying "plot" and a definitive resolution. I argue that the disjointed chronology and multiple narrators of the novel do not simply veil a conventional story line; instead, Pynchon thwarts expectations of metonymic coherence in order to emphasize relations of resemblance between past and present events, relations that his characters inevitably fail to recognize.

In chapter 3, "Purity as Parody in *The Crying of Lot 49*," I argue that Pynchon's most straightforward and conventionally "pure" narrative subverts its own sense of an ending by projecting dual conclusions that are in the strictest sense unimaginable. Although all the action seems to anticipate a climactic resolution that will either bestow absolute value and significance on the novel's world or affirm that neither value nor significance is possible, certain apparently nonessential or "waste" elements of the narrative turn out to have paramount importance.

Chapter 4, "The Arc and the Covenant: *Gravity's Rainbow* as Secular History," examines the ways in which the arc of the V-2 rocket, the "gravity's rainbow" of the title, serves as a metaphor for all linear, totalizing systems, including the "system" of the novel itself. The first section, " 'Structures Favoring Death,' " draws a parallel between the rocket's parabolic path and the path of providential history moving from its origin in the Fall to its terminus in apocalyptic annihilation, and suggests that the twentieth-century theory of a universe running down as it gains entropy is simply a revised version of the Christian myth, with the possibility of salvation removed. The second section, "Murphy's Law," points out the inadequacies that Pynchon finds in all such comprehensive explanatory schemata. No ordering principle can govern all aspects of reality because reality is not a single system, and Pynchon betrays his own apparent gravity—the high seriousness of his apparently nihilistic vision—by allowing the action of the novel to proliferate, thereby evading the control of the ostensible structure metaphor. The third section, "Narrative Theory and Practice," considers some of the comic implications of Pynchon's narrative strategies in this complex and yet immensely rewarding novel.

1

Including Middles

Thomas Pynchon writes difficult novels. His first, *V.*, which won the Faulkner Award for 1963, is even more ontologically unsettling than Faulkner's own *Absalom, Absalom!* in its refusal to offer a reconstructible "real story" underlying the layers of narrative discourse. *The Crying of Lot 49* (1966), though shorter and more immediately accessible, presents other grounds for confusion: what kind of concern are we supposed to feel for a protagonist named Oedipa Maas; which elements, if any, of the heavily satiric plot should we take seriously? His major work to date, *Gravity's Rainbow* (1973), has 760 pages, at least 300 individualized characters, and a tangle of plots so thoroughly contaminated by the naturalizing conventions of dream, hallucination, fantasy, film, theater, and interpolated texts that it is nearly impossible to say even in a provisional way what happens in it. The novels all celebrate diversity, multiplying situations, interrelationships, characters, voices, and attitudes with such abandon that they perplex understanding.

Thus the reader seeking his way is likely to welcome the suggestion, which runs through all three novels like Ariadne's thread, that this apparent diversity merely disguises an austere metaphysical binarism. Each of Pynchon's novels presents a fictional universe comprised of overlapping networks of codes and inhabited by at least one hermeneuticist who attempts to break these codes in order to reach a culminating revelation. These "critical" characters function as analogues to the

reader, piecing together bits of information to construct a coherent interpretation out of burgeoning intimations of inter-
connectedness. Each arrives at a reading of the evidence that
is at once structurally elegant and thematically despairing:
either "*everything is connected*"—in a cosmic conspiracy that
reduces individual agency to a pathetic delusion—or "nothing
is connected to anything, a condition not many of us can bear
for long."[1]

But to take the extremes of conspiratorial connectedness or
absolute unconnectedness as authorially sanctioned categories for interpreting the novels themselves is to reduce
Pynchon's complex patterns of iconography, allusion, and
metaphor to provisional structures that elude closure only
because closure would reveal their fundamental meaninglessness. If none of the books "comes to a conclusion" in conventional ways, the implication is that a conclusion would have to
affirm either that an externally imposed order renders individual life meaningless, or that the world is incomprehensibly
chaotic. Both conclusions would negate the significance of the
preceding action, an action that revolves around some character's quest after the meaning of his or her experience. If
Pynchon's three very different novels really center on the
choice between two versions of insignificance, they affirm
their own inconsequence.

I want to suggest, on the contrary, that though Pynchon
does indeed dichotomize possibilities in all three novels,
"order" and "chaos" are not his own "authorized" categories for describing reality. He is both more playful and more
duplicitous than such reductions can acknowledge. Furthermore, his issues are less metaphysical than epistemological, in
that he offers the familiar opposition, not to affirm that reality
is rigidly ordered or intolerably chaotic, but to dramatize the
absolutist discourse that governs the way people think about
reality. Each of his "critical" characters inevitably arrives at
an impasse when his reconstructing activities lead him to the
familiar antitheses: the world is either formed or formless,

meaningful or meaningless, orderly or chaotic, a unified system or a jumble of random components. But, I shall argue, it is remarkable how few of the novels' proliferating implications are covered by either pole of the antithesis.

Pynchon's questing characters begin with the assumption that, as the *Gravity's Rainbow* narrator puts it, "*everything is connected*," and that consequently their discoveries constitute aspects of a single truth about the shape and direction of cosmic history. At some point, however, they are forced to reflect on the status of such connections. The question is always whether inferred relations are somehow inherent in reality or whether they are imposed by a consciousness that cannot "bear for long" a condition in which "nothing is connected to anything." Real relations and imagined relations turn out to have equally ominous implications. If the relations are real, they constitute an ironic argument from design testifying to the existence of a malign or at least antihuman designer—known as Them in *Gravity's Rainbow*, the Tristero in *The Crying of Lot 49*, and V. in *V*. In this case, if the quest does get at the truth about the way things are, the truth is that human beings are completely under the control of outside forces. Knowledge is not power but proof of impotence, and under the circumstances it may be just as well not to know. If the relations are imaginary, on the other hand, the quest reveals nothing but a desire to discern connections among a random assembly of wholly unrelated details. If there is pathos in this recognition, there is also despair, for inquiry is perpetually deprived of its object and locked in its own sterile cogitations. The questing hero becomes the paranoid, intuiting connections out of his own need for order and unable even to share his delusory experience.

The protagonists of all three books confront these alternatives. Tyrone Slothrop in *Gravity's Rainbow* vacillates between paranoia and antiparanoia until he begins to disintegrate. Oedipa Maas in *The Crying of Lot 49* waits "for a symmetry of choices to break down, to go skew" (p. 136) and make room for some "middle" between the absolute reality and the absolute unreality of her totalizing principle, the Tristero. Herbert Stencil in *V.* weighs his evidence, finds that it points either to a plot that engulfs him or to the fact that he has tried to "exhume an hallucination" (p. 421), and begins to repeat obsessively, "Events seem to be ordered into an ominous logic" (p. 423). The persistent opposition is extremely ominous, and Pynchon keeps returning to it to ring new changes on the Sophoclean theme of knowledge as tragedy.

The problem with such "ominous logic," however, is that it is not particularly logical. There is an infinite "middle" region between the hyperbolic extremes of an absolute, externally imposed (i.e., a particular kind of) order and total chaos, and Pynchon's novels inhabit this "middle" region. For instance, when Oedipa realizes that her interpretations of the experiential "legacy" bequeathed to her by Pierce Inverarity have narrowed to two thoroughly unpalatable alternatives, the narrator of *Lot 49* observes, "She had heard all about excluded middles; they were bad shit, to be avoided . . . " (p. 136). The principle of excluded middles, a fundamental axiom in logic, maintains that if a proposition is false, its contradictory must be true, and vice versa (if it is false that cows have wings, it is true that cows do not have wings); there is no "middle" ground between them. Following this principle, Oedipa concludes that if the enigmatic Tristero exists, it infuses her world with meaning and value, but that if the Tristero does not exist, meaning and value are impossibilities.

> For it was now like walking among matrices of a great digital computer, the zeroes and ones twinned above, hanging like balanced mobiles right and left, ahead, thick, maybe endless. Behind the hieroglyphic streets there would either be a transcendent meaning, or only the earth. In the songs Miles, Dean, Serge and Leonard sang was either some fraction of the truth's numinous beauty . . . or only a power spectrum. Tremaine the Swastika Salesman's reprieve from holocaust was either an injustice, or the absence of a wind. . . . Either Oedipa in the orbiting ecstacy of a true paranoia, or a real Tristero. (Pp. 136–37)

But this formulation of the dilemma obscures the fact that the binary alternatives are not true contradictories; they do not exhaust the possibilities. In the course of her quest, Oedipa has construed her discoveries as intimations of a sacred and transcendent order, and in the process she has been drawn into the assumption that these discoveries will be absolutely meaningless if such an order does not exist. In the absence of some version of an omnipotent providence, even a parodic and whimsically vengeful version, she believes the world must be "really," if incomprehensibly, chaotic. But the great irony of the novel is that her quest has an importance apart from any final baptism of transcendent significance. The novel ends without "coming to a conclusion" about whether the Tristero does or does not exist because any such conclusion would be beside the point. The novel is thematically and aesthetically whole apart from any supposedly climactic resolution.

The real significance of these dichotomies is pointed up by the narrator's comment on Oedipa's "excluded middles." The narrator does not address the question of which alternative is preferable or which is correct; instead he asks how the options got so limited: "and how had it ever happened here, with the chances once so good for diversity?" (p. 136). How did the proposed interpretations of experience dwindle to two unlivable positions? Logically, the principle of excluded middles does not justify this reduction, for the contradictory of "everything is connected" is "*not* everything is connected," a proposition that leaves ample room for the possibility that some things are connected, and in innumerably different ways. In raising the order/chaos antithesis, Pynchon encourages a habit of thinking that cannot tolerate the instability and complexity of multiple patterns of interrelation. All his books insist that this habit of thinking is analogous to conventional expectations of narrative coherence.

One of Pynchon's central insights is that people tend to "read" experience the same way that they read books. A novel is traditionally a totalizing structure that derives much of its energy from its promise to reveal the intrinsic connections uniting apparently contingent elements. Terms like "plot" and "development" suggest the ways in which the action is teleological, directed toward attaining an end, whereas terms like "resolution" and "conclusion" indicate that the end of a narrative has affinities with the terminus of an argument. A conventional narrative is a process of putting things together, and the satisfaction of closure involves the sense that everything has been definitively wrapped up. When Stencil begins to piece together V-words in accordance with his thesis that such signifiers are aspects of "one and the same V.," when Oedipa infers that the factor common to all the arcane information she discovers is an association with the Tristero, when Slothrop begins to accumulate evidence from his past that links him to the V-2 rocket, these characters are assembling elements of experience in narrative order. The quest promises to proceed by accretion, with each incident building on the last and providing another piece of data toward a revelation of the whole pattern. The process of bringing events to a climax merges with the process of discovering the essential truth about reality, so that the lure of closure is clearly identified with the lure of totality. As a disembodied spirit summoned to a séance in *Gravity's Rainbow* reports, "Here it's possible to see the whole shape at once" (p. 165). In anticipating such a conclusion, the questing characters look forward to occupying a vantage outside their experience, a vantage that will give them an authorized perspective on the "whole shape at once."

The problem, of course, is that such characters find themselves irrevocably inside the stories they construct, so that in various ways the end of the narrative threatens to finish them. "Approach and avoid" becomes Stencil's motto when he realizes that if he finds the historical force he calls V., her presence will guarantee the entropic dissolution of the society he represents. Oedipa herself becomes the "excluded middle" when she understands that a real Tristero might just as well destroy her for recognizing its existence as exalt her to unimaginable heights of "Meaning," whereas an imagined Tristero will establish both that her life is meaningless and that she is insane.[2] Slothrop assesses his position in the plot and decides that either a malevolent quasi-authorial presence is directing him toward an unknown but probably fatal "end," or that his wanderings have no direction at all: "Either They have put him here for a reason, or he's just here. He isn't sure that he wouldn't, actually, rather have that *reason . . .* " (p. 434). Such incidents contrive to suggest that any "order" in reality will necessarily be the kind of narrative form in which events accrete toward a revelatory, "conclusive" conclusion. But if life has this kind of narrative form, it will reveal its significance *only* when it concludes, and this fact can provide little comfort to characters who by definition cannot get outside the text of their experience. And if life does not have such narrative form—if it does not build to a climactic insight—it is meaningless. Or so it seems, once "order" becomes synonymous with narrative order—or "plot."

In constructing his novels, Pynchon seems especially concerned to parody this widespread, if tacit, assumption that meaning is the culmination of an exhaustive series of discoveries, that truth is what everything adds up to. His characters soon learn that they cannot separate personal from public significance, so that in looking for the meaning of their discoveries, they find themselves involved with heady metaphysical problems: the meaning of life, of history, of humanity. Their own lives become elements in a larger continuum; in "plotting" experience they find themselves tracing the curve of historical development, a curve that follows a classical pattern of plot construction in rising only to fall.[3] By making their own experiences the consequence of a long historical buildup, they effectively locate the "rising action" in the past. Both *V.* and *Gravity's Rainbow* play explicitly on the notion that the climax has already occurred, and that at some retrospective point on the time-line, history took an irreversible downward turn. In both of these books, the plunge toward annihilation was precipitated by a rising technology, which grew like Frankenstein's creature to dominate its creators.[4] In *Lot 49* the focus is more restricted. Only America seems bent on self-destruction, and the downward curve is less steep, leading to a progressively more fragmented and banal culture that promises to suffocate people in their own waste.

Pynchon finds an analogy for such "plots" in the vision of universal rundown suggested by the second law of thermodynamics. This law gives physical processes an ironic goal in a state of terminal "heat-death." In universalizing this law so that it applies to history, characters claim scientific sanction for their intuitions that things will inevitably get worse. By offering the second law as an explanatory principle that can account for social phenomena, Pynchon underscores the human tendency to suppose that history has a determinate "shape." In the vacuum left when the providential system for directing history toward an end point fell into general disfavor, science appeared to offer a model of universal connectedness that would contain time in a narrative pattern—that would give history a beginning, a middle, and an end. The irony is that this revised version of the providential schema contained no loopholes allowing for a resolution in divine comedy. If time has a "shape," it reveals human history as a being-toward-death, and there can be no redemption, no dispensation in which human beings are translated into transcendent beings who look down on the whole drama from outside. Pynchon makes the providential plot the type of all attempts to make sense out of the world by giving events narrative coherence.[5] This plot lurks as an unacknowledged paradigm behind the idea that experience accretes toward a terminal revelation.

By allowing each of his novels to entertain the polarized theses that the world is either a rigid, preordained order or else a concatenation of random, unrelated details, Pynchon dramatizes the vacuity of conceiving experience as plotted and of meaning as resulting only from a culminating synthesis. He does this by exploiting the seductiveness of these two theses, provoking the reader to accept them and thereby to discover how effectively they rule out "middles." The argument that if everything in creation cannot be accounted for within an all-embracing "plot," then there is no order at all rules out the "middles" between these extremes: the possibility of local meaning-systems that claim to be partial reflections of reality—novels, for instance.[6] But Pynchon's novels themselves are "middles," and they demonstrate how much significance can be included within a plurality of limited, contingent, overlapping systems that coexist and form relations with one another without achieving abstract intellectual closure.

Pynchon's narrative strategy is based on a tension essential to the novel as a genre; not coincidentally, he finds this tension essential to a modernist mode of being in the world. On the one hand, everything seems oriented toward a future synthesis that will comprehend all apparent contingencies. The narrative present appears to be a condition of lack or need, and thus reaching forward for its destined fulfillment. This teleological thrust generates energy out of the sense of purposiveness. One of Pynchon's most evocative expressions for this tendency comes from *Gravity's Rainbow*, where he calls it "Holy-Center-Approaching." On the other hand, no promise of synthetic resolution seems adequate to the proliferating implications that the present offers. Precisely because the present lacks unity, it leaves room for unanticipated developments. As long as burgeoning meanings do not converge at a Holy Center, further meanings are possible. The absence of a definitive synthetic unity is finally a condition for freedom, and Pynchon plays on a further conclusion: such an absence is also an enabling condition for language, and especially for the language of his novels.

"Holy-Center-Approaching"

Holy-Center-Approaching is soon to be the number one Zonal pastime. Its balmy heyday is nearly on it. Soon more champions, adepts, magicians of all ranks and orders will be in the field than ever before in the history of the game. The sun will rule all enterprise, if it be honest and sporting. The Gauss curve will herniate toward the excellent. And tankers the likes of Närrisch and Slothrop here will have already been weeded out. (*GR*, p. 508)

In the phrase "Holy-Center-Approaching," the narrator of *Gravity's Rainbow* encapsulates the formula of the quest romance. The Holy Center is the terminus of the quest, the epiphanic point in both time and space where the questing hero realizes the full meaning of his search, life, and world. It is thus the conclusion toward which the narrative tends. In Pynchon's books no major character reaches this Holy Center. The pattern of the quest is an infinite approach, one that brings the seeker closer and closer to a terminal revelation without allowing him to reach it. In the passage quoted above, Slothrop, the quintessential bumbler, and Närrisch, the victimized technician (whose name translates as "foolish"), are two Parsifal-types in *Gravity's Rainbow*. Both have experiences in which (the narrator strongly suggests) they ought to arrive at a full understanding of what everything adds up to. Both, however, remain unenlightened. Both miss the message and consequently remain outside a privileged circle of "champions, adepts, magicians of all ranks and orders." Failure to achieve revelation is a hallmark of Pynchon's questing heroes. This failure seems to doom such characters to a sort of tragic schlemielhood—Tchitcherine in the same novel "will miss the Light, but not the Finger" (p. 566).

This asymptotic approach toward an unavailable center, or central insight, is common to all three novels and helps give Pynchon's writing its peculiarly enigmatic quality. Because no narrator intervenes to explain just what, exactly, a character has missed seeing, the reader finds himself in the company of the schlemiels, inexplicably removed from the knowledge that should explain how everything fits together. The novels all capitalize on a sense of insufficiency. By creating this sense of insufficiency, Pynchon has effectively created a gap that appears to require filling.

If Pynchon were a more conventional writer, these provocative openings in the text would function as invitations, encouraging readers to apply their own powers of reasoning in order to establish what is missing. The result would be a type of hermetic reading, beginning from the premise that the supposedly withheld central truth is so cunningly encoded in the text that it requires translation. When this is the case, it is the reader who must become the champion, adept, and magician, teasing out the meaning that ironically debased characters are incapable of reaching.

But this hermetic approach to Pynchon's novels is comparable to an approach to Conrad that begins with the question, "What *is* the heart of darkness?" It is possible to argue for any number of answers to this question, but argument is pointless when no answer satisfies. Similarly in Pynchon's case, proposed explications are invariably inadequate to the promise of revelation that his mysteries generate. Furthermore, if the gaps are there to be filled, it is odd that there have been so many contradictory interpretations of Pynchon's central thesis, for of course contradictory results are unacceptable to a theory that begins from the premise that the author himself has hidden the sole sanctioned interpretation.[7]

Another way of reading Pynchon's novels also begins from the sense of insufficiency and failed revelation: such a reading concludes that the gaps are unavoidable because Pynchon's central insight is intrinsically inexpressible. Language, in this view, is simply inadequate to the truth, although the truth is thinkable: one can know something without being able to speak or write it. It follows that the novels are attempts to create conditions favorable to revelation, i.e., in some manner to signify that-which-cannot-be-signified, although because they are linguistic structures they fall short of revelation themselves.[8]

This way of reading has the advantage of respecting Pynchon's absences and silences, but presumes at the outset that language and meaning are independent and that the most essential kinds of meaning exist apart from, and out of the reach of, language—a thesis currently arousing intense controversy among philosophers, linguists, and literary theorists.[9] Although it is possible that Pynchon himself subscribes to a theory that dichotomizes language and meaning, and that he genuinely has something in mind that he is unable to put in words, I am not sure that we can assign either of these opinions to him on the evidence of his fictional writings. Certainly his novels engage in a rhetoric of absence and loss, and his narrators regularly mourn their inability to express precisely what is most important. But there are also inescapable ironies in the spectacle of a richly variegated prose lamenting its own inadequacy. And methodologically this approach troubles me because, in accepting at face value the claim that language is incapable of expressing central truths, it tends to focus on what is *not* being said. Thus it deflects attention from the question of what Pynchon gains by insisting on language's failure. What he gains, I think, is a structural trope that reconciles the reader to what might otherwise be an intolerable profusion of voices, characters, relations, and themes. By raising and keeping open the question of an unavailable insight, Pynchon is able to sustain expectation while warding off the easy supposition that his pluralistic fictional universes mirror chaos.

Pynchon uses this trope of the unavailable insight as a strategy to exploit the widespread belief that things ought to add up, even if they do not. His questing characters make connections in the anticipation that eventually everything will have a place in a single, fully coherent scheme, and they discover local and contingent relationships in the process of straining toward this final explanation. They act as exempla for the reader because they exemplify a tendency in Western culture. In Pynchon's comic vision, Western man is a failed platonist, committed to the proposition that the truth is One, and able to function only because he keeps happening on truths on the way toward the elusive Truth. People take note of diversity by trying to resolve it into unity. By the same token, Pynchon's novels promise to add up in order to call attention to the complex ways in which they do *not* add up. Articulating an important concern of modernism, Yeats wrote, "Things fall apart; the centre cannot hold; / Mere anarchy is loosed upon the world." Pynchon is sensitive to the psychological persuasiveness of Yeats's leap from one extreme to the other and makes use of Yeats's version of the order/chaos opposition—that in the absence of a center everything must be "mere anarchy." He constructs his radically decentralized texts around the premise that the center is unaccountably missing. It should be there, he grants. Undoubtedly it was there at one time, or it would not be so sorely missed. The longing for unity, then, is a cosmic nostalgia, a desire to return to an original state.

By introducing the idea of an unavailable center, or central insight, Pynchon provides a myth of origins for both a complex and unpredictable reality and a language that proliferates uncontrollably. This myth commands imaginative assent because in essence it is the myth of the Fall, conflated with Gnostic, Kabbalist, platonist, and scientific traditions for additional resonance. This Fall marks the disintegration of an original center and the beginning of history—a history that starts in order to end, following the providential model. Pynchon thus opens up the space of narrative, the "middle" region between origin and ending that his novels occupy. He also motivates increasing diversity by making it an attempt to recover unity. Reality divides amoeba-like into new manifestations, multiplying its interrelationships endlessly in the attempt to recover its lost oneness, as words split, recombine, split again in the futile effort to recover the redemptive Word. And naïve readers follow the spirals and whorls of the plot in anticipation that everything will add up, even when the novels' own rhetoric seems to guarantee that the end product of such an adding up can only be tragedy.

The naïve reader's anticipation that all these different aspects of the novels will add up to an insight mirrors the search each questing character undertakes. The convention of novelistic coherence encourages the reader to assume that certain characters will be more important than others, that certain details will emerge as significant and others will remain so much window dressing, that the narrators' observations will come to constitute a pattern from which a limited set of statements comprising the novel's meaning can be drawn. But the novels resist efforts to subordinate some parts to others in the interests of a comprehensible coherence. Pynchon is able to sustain multiple emphases by loading the *promise* of insight to come with more connotations than any set of determinate meaning-statements could conceivably bear, and then deferring fulfillment of this promise beyond the conclusions of the books. The trope of the unavailable insight thus allows all three books to end before they can "come to a conclusion." Because the novels embody a promise of revelation, the thematic "conclusion"—the articulation of what this all means—haunts each book as something that is not there.

Of course, the promise of such "conclusions," such summings-up, is also a threat. The novels are filled with warnings that the unity that results from making all the connections is a trap. The questing characters who try to connect their discoveries have to face the prospect that they too are connected, in a system that transcends their control. Herbert Stencil beings to fear that the mysterious V. is so much the century's Big One that if he ever finds out the truth about the symbol, he will be taken over by its decadent and entropic evocations. Oedipa Maas suspects that the Tristero's malignancy and omnipresence guarantee her destruction. And in *Gravity's Rainbow* connection is always allied with the possibility that a ubiquitous They manipulate all the people and events of the novel's world. But the attendant implication—that too much connection is dangerous—presumes that it is *possible* to resolve diversity into unambiguous unity. In each of the novels, Pynchon plays in a different way on a theme that parodies the modernist dream of totalization implicit in

Forster's "only connect": that the process of making connections only raises further complexities, and that the perception of multiple levels of interrelationship works against the expectation of a synthetic, revelatory conclusion.

Readings like the "hermetic" one I mentioned above, which regard a synthetic, revelatory conclusion as somehow latent in the text, inadvertently underscore the insufficiency of any such conclusion. To attach names like "entropy" or "decadence" to the V-symbol in *V.* is to limit the resonance of that symbol to a certain frequency, and part of the mystery (and the humor) of *V.* comes from the way V. functions as a free-floating signifier with a potentially inexhaustible range of reference. In attaching multiple levels of connotation to an initial, Pynchon plays on the convention that an initial synecdochically "stands for" something—usually some word beginning with that initial (although the Roman numeral five creeps easily under the rubric, and at least one intrepid reviewer has suggested that V. is a truncated, inverted "A," which opens the door to an enormous number of additional linguistic referents).[10] The symbol is so overdetermined that all of its manifestations in the novel seem only distortions or approximations of an ultimate core of significance. Entropy and decadence are large concepts, but they do not banish the mystery of the central symbol; they fall far short of the magnitude of its implied message. As the novel proceeds, V. comes to promise so much that any resolution to the quest would seem ludicrously deficient.

Yet the symbol never gets a range of reference so limitless that the question of what V. "stands for" becomes completely meaningless. V. remains the object of the search as the novel closes with the unexplained death of Sidney Stencil, and everything suggests that to explain V. would be to explain the elder Stencil's death and all else that, within the multiple narrative frames, somehow "happens." All of the separate, limited manifestations of V. in the novel point to the idea that the truth about V. cannot be expressed in language; but because

V. somehow exists beyond the text, so completely whole that language is always inadequate to express it, all of these manifestations can coexist. Much of the fascination of the book arises from the fact that the various characters, voices, and incidents have so *little* conventional narrative connection to one another. Yet because they all are associated with V. by relations of juxtaposition and resemblance, they participate in the charisma of the unavailable insight that V. somehow "stands for." All somehow point back to it—point back, as if they had it as their common origin, as if the insight had generated all of them. For the novel presents itself as radically incomplete, "radically" in the sense that it is unable to recover its origins. Because Pynchon's working premise is that the unavailable insight cannot be incarnated in language, this insight appears to have exfoliated an incredible variety of manifestations—the V-words in *V.* These manifestations, the novel contrives to suggest, are unified only by virtue of their origin in, and their reference to, a common source.

In his second novel, *The Crying of Lot 49*, Pynchon plays more explicitly than in *V.* with the conventions of traditional linear narrative. As questing hero, Oedipa Maas is concerned to discover a central symbol called the Tristero; and since her perspective is the only one the book offers, there is less overt suggestion of alternatives to a quest for a terminal revelation— "terminal" in that revelation threatens to terminate not only the quest but also the quester. In approved detective story fashion, Oedipa accumulates clues that point to the Tristero but thereby compound the mystery, for the Tristero itself is a signifier. She anticipates encountering the Tristero "in its terrible nakedness," but it is not the organization itself that is crucial to her quest; it is the message the Tristero can deliver.

> Would it smile, then, be coy, and would it flirt away harmlessly backstage, say goodnight with a Bourbon Street bow and leave her in peace? Or would it instead, the dance ended, come back down the runway, its luminous stare locked to Oedipa's, smile gone malign and pitiless; bend to her alone among the desolate

rows of seats and begin to speak words she never wanted to hear?
(P. 36)

The manifestations of the Tristero prove inadequate to this
anticipation. Oedipa's search—and her research, for she is
one of Pynchon's more literary detectives—explicate the long
history of an underground resistance movement that seems to
exist for the purpose of providing different ways to communicate information. The concept of communication is fertile in
this novel, and the implication is that different means of communication will yield different messages. Yet Oedipa never
receives "the words she never wanted to hear"; she never
gets the message, although it seems to lurk somewhere beyond
the formal conclusion of the novel. As she collects information
about the Tristero itself, she routinizes its charisma, to adopt
the phrase that Pynchon himself borrows from Max Weber.
The Tristero becomes more and more a historical phenomenon, operating always in the shadow of legitimate postal services. It appears capable of sabotaging established systems of
communication in bizarre and often inexplicable ways, and of
killing investigators who come too close to revealing its existence, but it finally does not constitute a message. And in the
context of the promised message, even the most malevolent
manifestations of the Tristero seem inadequate, even trivial.
All of these manifestations emphasize the idea of communication while failing to articulate what it is that must be communicated. The failure of these manifestations to produce meaning
reinforces the implication that the anticipated message cannot
be communicated by traditional means: not in the novel, not in
language. Once again, the trope of the unavailable insight
allows the promise of ultimate meaning to remain open at the
close of the narrative.

The absent insight generates an unprecedented variety of
quests and questing characters in *Gravity's Rainbow*, which
also contains some of the most explicit references to the failure of language to reveal what should mean the most. If
Stencil's ploy is "approach and avoid" and Oedipa simply

approaches, in the hope and fear that revelation will seize her, Tchitcherine, Enzian, and Slothrop are faced with the prospect of an approach that is infinite. The gap between language and its true referent may be miniscule but cannot be bridged. In a startling passage describing Slothrop's flagging efforts at Holy-Center-Approaching, the narrator switches suddenly into direct address, and the extension of his "you" seems to encompass not only Slothrop but all the characters, the reader, and even the author:

> But just over the embankment, down in the arena, what might that have been just now, waiting in this broken moonlight, camouflage paint from fins to point crazed into jigsaw . . . is it, then, really never to find you again? Not even in your worst times of night, with pencil words on your page only Δt from the things they stand for? And inside the victim is twitching, fingering beads, touching wood, avoiding any Operational Word. Will it really never come to take you, now? (P. 510; Pynchon's ellipsis)

This passage introduces the idea that reference necessarily involves a lack. Words and "the things they stand for" never connect; words always remain "delta-t" from their referents, and the allusion to the fractional divisions of the infinitesimal calculus implies that language can pour endlessly into the vacuum without filling it. Like the "frames" that the German technicians at Peenemünde used to study the trajectory of the rocket, words multiply distinctions endlessly without ever constituting a whole. A succession of "frames" can only counterfeit motion; there is always an infinite number of delta-t's between one frame and the next. An endless stream of words can only approach infinitely closer to the coincidence with the referent that might be revelation. Failed revelation haunts the whole novel. *Gravity's Rainbow* presents itself as poised eternally on the "leading edge" of insight. Yet the novel is not rendered meaningless, on its own terms, by this premise of failure. It is full of implications precisely because revelation has not come to take it, because it has been passed over—because, in short, of its preterition.

According to Calvinist doctrine, preterition is the condition of having been passed over by God. Because they exist outside the redemptive system, the Preterite should be meaningless by definition: there is no place for them in the divine scheme of things. But Tyrone Slothrop's heretical ancestor, William Slothrop, argued in his treatise *On Preterition* that "Elect" and "Preterite" are co-implicative terms: one can be defined only by reference to the other. He went on to maintain that the Preterite are as important to God as the Elect, for the Preterite exist to define what the Elect are not. As Pynchon's narrator chortles, "You can bet the Elect in Boston were pissed off about that" (p. 555).

The linguistic structure that is *Gravity's Rainbow* is self-defined by its own preterition, by the premise that revelation has passed it over. At the same time, it creates a sense of this absent revelation through its pointing, through successive linguistic approximations that claim to fall short of the missing unity.[11] In terms of the unavailable insight, the novel is a failure, infinitely approaching but never achieving the indivisible unity it "stands for." But because the novel itself has defined this unity as what is missing, it embodies the absence of unity as something unity can never be: as fecundity, as multiple versions of "Holy-Center-Approaching," as a plenitude of failed revelations.

Gravity's Rainbow provides the clearest illustration of the use Pynchon makes of the trope of the absent insight, but the trope is common to all three novels and provides the context within which all three novels take shape. The premise that the center is missing, and that the novels insistently and incessantly "point toward" because the ultimate object of reference is denied them, creates a space in which Pynchon can realize multiple possibilities simultaneously. Because the Holy Center, the ultimate guarantor of meaning, is unavailable in the novels, the novels occupy a context in which any number of local systems of meaning can coexist. Language cannot signify originating unity: words are always delta-t from the "things they stand for," doomed, within Pynchon's fictional worlds, to signify only each other and to run the risk inherent in "only connect," the risk of connecting so completely that human freedom becomes defined as an illusion. But total connectedness of this sort is only one possibility for a language that is deprived of—or freed from—the necessity of referring to a single, ultimate source. It is one of an infinite number of possibilities. The absence of the center opens up a space in which freedom creates and explores its own prospects, and by postulating an unavailable referent, Pynchon can allow the resulting play of language to generate multiple versions of meaning and value. His novels, like his characters, are obsessed with connections, but none of the novels adds up to a single idea of order. Each subverts oversimplification by dramatizing multiple, overlapping, and often contradictory ideas of order that express the human effort to find intelligibility in experiences.

Absence, Language, and Freedom

The trope of the absent center supplies the motive for making patterns out of language. The promise of meaning, even a meaning endlessly deferred, compels Pynchon's characters (and his readers) to look for possible connections between the objects and events that comprise their experience. Every phantom resemblance, every unforeseen happening, could be a link in the chain leading to the Holy Center, the center that so obstinately refuses to be revealed. In Pynchon's novels human beings try to construct meanings because the premise that the center did not hold constitutes an original loss. The particles of experience to be connected thus become fragments of an original unity. The search for meaning is the consquence of the failure of revelation:

> The rest of us, not chosen for enlightenment, left on the outside of Earth, at the mercy of a Gravity we have only begun to learn how to detect and measure, must go on blundering inside our

front-brain faith in Kute Korrespondences, hoping that for each
psi-synthetic taken from Earth's soul there is a molecule, secular,
more or less ordinary and named, over here—kicking endlessly
among the plastic trivia, finding in each Deeper Significance and
trying to string them all together like terms of a power series
hoping to zero in on the tremendous and secret Function whose
name, like the permuted names of God, cannot be spoken... (*GR*,
p. 590; Pynchon's ellipsis)

As this passage suggests, the search for meaning could not
occur if the searchers were not aware of the possibility of
enlightenment, of the "tremendous and secret Function
whose name, like the permuted names of God, cannot be
spoken." But the search must articulate connections, in the
dual sense of setting such connections apart and of speaking
them. The condition of articulation, which governs the secular
worlds of the novels, guarantees that the indivisible, silent
center will remain always out of reach. Language can only
divide, recombine, violate the perfection of silence with the
noisy incompleteness of always saying. Yet saying means.
Although Pynchon's novels depend on the premise of center-
lessness, they use this premise in an original way. Centerless-
ness is not so much a theme, finally, as a condition, the given
in Pynchon's fictional worlds that makes action, and writing,
possible.

In the theological terminology of *Gravity's Rainbow*, words
remain an infinite distance from the Word. It is no accident
that Pynchon's experiments with withheld meaning led him to
adopt the technical language of Christian theology, and
specifically of Calvinism, for Western culture traditionally expresses concern with an ultimate reality existing beyond the
possibility of signification in terms of transcendence. If be-
lievers could attach the name of God to this ultimate reality,
they also insisted that they could not conceive of God's nature. Even Saint Thomas Aquinas, in his endeavor to reconcile faith and reason, declared that divine attributes could only
be predicated by analogy, and that the transcendent term of

the analogy remained entirely incomprehensible to human reason.[12] For the American Puritans, who form part of the historical backdrop of *Gravity's Rainbow*, the sign of a transcendent God was manifested in an act of grace—through the Word made words in God's own Text. The Puritans became hermeneuticists who sifted scriptural analogies for the radical terms. Their enterprise was risky because only the Elect could arrive at revelation. But revelation was also a *sign* of election—if, of course, it was revelation and not some perverted and heretical reading of the data. The entire Puritan enterprise attests to a faith that transcendence can become immanence, absence can become presence, words can become the Word— at least for those singled out to be recipients of revelation. The gap could be bridged, the Puritans believed; but it could only be bridged with supernatural assistance. The "bookish kind of reflex" that leads Slothrop to "hear quote marks in the speech of others" derives from a tradition of "earlier Slothrops packing Bibles around the blue hilltops as part of their gear, memorizing chapter and verse the structures of Arks, Temples, Visionary Thrones—all the materials and dimensions. Data behind which always, nearer or farther, was the numinous certainty of God" (pp. 241–42).

By the time Tyrone Slothrop, the last Puritan of his line and possessor of a more unsettling kind of reflex, starts analyzing the data, however, it is less certain who or what lies behind. Election is a dubious concept in *Gravity's Rainbow*, associated always with manipulation and control, the earmarks of Them. The Puritan God who saves and damns without discernible criteria appears as the last distorted trace of an inexpressible presence that was once center, origin, and guarantor of what irreducibly is. All three books express nostalgia and a desire to "get back" to a sort of primal oneness. Yet the language of the novels flies from this center, as the images of the diaspora and the expanding universe in *Gravity's Rainbow* illustrate. Within Pynchon's fictional worlds, language's hypothesized origin is this unifying presence, but language becomes language only when presence withdraws into the mythic past—into absence. If language has an origin, this origin precedes language and is unavailable to it. In its multiplicity and diversity, language excludes presence:

> Is there a single root, deeper than anyone has probed, from which Slothrop's Blackwords only appear to flower separately? Or has he by way of the language caught the German mania for namegiving, dividing the Creation finer and finer, analyzing, setting namer more hopelessly apart from named, even to bringing in the mathematics of combination, tacking together established nouns to get new ones, the insanely, endlessly diddling play of a chemist whose molecules are words.... (*GR*, p. 391; Pynchon's ellipsis)

In this passage Pynchon links the modernist metaphor of the disintegrating center to the phenomenon of language. Language diversifies and proliferates endlessly, "dividing the Creation finer and finer, analyzing, setting namer more hopelessly apart from named." Yet the fact of language seems to point back to an original Creation, an original named. Words carry within themselves intimations of their own incompleteness, and tend to suggest "a single root, deeper than anyone has probed." It is ultimately the desire to return to this root that prompts the "chemist whose molecules are words" to create artificial bonds until he has synthesized a unity of his own, an explanatory structure that will connect the linguistic atoms of his shattered Creation.

But no explanatory structure, however comprehensive, can recapture the unity of the broken center, a center that is not just crumbling but simply does not exist. "Center," "source," "origin," "root," "Creation," "named"—all of these terms occur within the hazily nostalgic context of a mythic past. Language is all that is left, and words themselves must be strung together in molecular chains if anything is to make sense. The novels take place in the aftermath of the explosion that released language to divide, proliferate, and recombine in its "endlessly diddling play." There can be no getting back to unity. And according to this apocalyptic vision of language as Fall, the promised end can only be annihilation. Yet the novels do not span this implied stretch of providential history. Instead, Pynchon's fictions inhabit the boundless space between the originating One of a postulated primal unity and the terminating Zero that is the end of time: the space of language and the freedom of language to constitute worlds.

As linguistic constructions, Pynchon's fictions cannot figure forth a "reality" that either precedes or antedates language. Both the One and the Zero are limiting cases. They constitute a myth that circumscribes the fact of language, but within language they do not signify: signification implies language. Within the worlds of Pynchon's novels, language is the matter out of which meanings must be compounded, and its "endlessly diddling play" must produce all the coherence and value that these worlds can have.

All three novels thus sustain a tension between two opposing attitudes toward language. On the one hand, the central fact of language is its inadequacy. Language cannot signify beyond itself, and in its efforts to transcend itself it proliferates endlessly, producing a multiplicity of structures that refer in increasingly complex ways to each other without coming any closer to a "reality" that can be defined only by its imperviousness to signification. On the other hand, there is a kind of perverseness in attaching the name "reality" to a state of ignorance, to an inexplicable something that is precisely what is not the case in a world where all possible meanings must be made of language. If language is the condition of the only experience that is possible within the novels, it is absurd to strain after a "reality" beyond the reach of words. The space of the fallen world is also the space of radical freedom, and the challenge is to produce versions of coherence out of the fact that words signify each other. Meaning must emerge from the play of language, or it will not emerge at all. In the absence of an external guarantor of truth, human beings must constitute fictions to address their needs for meaning and value. The capacity of language to proliferate endlessly serves the enterprise of creating new fictions, each in its own way a response to the demand for a supreme fiction, none of them able to maintain supremacy.

Yet Pynchon's novels always embody a quixotic stance toward language, and this stance allows the two attitudes—the attitude that views language as fallen and the attitude that views language as freedom—to interact. The impetus to create fictions is always in some way the attempt to reclaim the lost unity, or to imitate it in a linguistic structure so consistent and inclusive that there is no room for further fictions. Explanatory structures that begin as a human response to the absence of an authoritative presence come to be taken for center, origin, unity, absolute reality. Cultural constructs become governing premises. The idea of an originating and divine authority that sanctions all imputations of meaning and value to the world translates into a tyranny of explanatory structures.

Pynchon's novels simultaneously explore and parody this longing to pull things together, to form the matter of language into a global fiction of such Parmenidean perfection that alternatives become impossible. A completely coherent fiction would create a sense of complete inevitability, in which everything happens as it must happen. In their various ways, the inhabitants of Pynchon's universes aspire toward such complete coherence when they try to constitute the events of their lives into intelligible sequences and to make these intelligible sequences the definition of who they are and what their place is in a coherent and intelligible world. In such a fiction, everything would be accounted for, everything would have a place, and every event would be explained in terms of a preceding event, for the drive to make meaning out of the world can easily, and almost imperceptibly, turn into the compulsion to make the world totally coherent and explicable. Every "why," according to this extreme version of coherence, would have to be answerable with the same kind of "because": in order to link the atoms of experience together, Pynchon's characters and narrators look for causes. In this enterprise they resemble the classical physicist who aims to trace all the phenomena of his world to a system of laws, or the traditional novelist who is supremely concerned to make his novels "come out"—to satisfy totally the naïve reader's expectation that apparent contingencies will all come to be understood as inevitabilities. According to this extreme version of coherence, experience must be reducible to a self-contained system, and the glue that holds such a system together is the assumption that a sufficient cause can be found for every event. The inhabitants of Pynchon's worlds continually try to exchange their freedom for the security of a wholly coherent causal explanation.

In this way the yearning to find causes becomes a symptom of a primordial nostalgia for the absent, originating Center. Tyrone Slothrop's search for his identity, for instance, is a search for the cause of his mysterious erections. His quest leads him to what the narrator terms a Holy Center, the launching site of the V-2 rocket that has his number—and this number is 00000. Slothrop's identity seems tied up with this fivefold negation, and the whole enterprise of explaining Slothrop that concerns so many of the characters of *Gravity's Rainbow* seems similarly concerned to negate Slothrop by reducing him to an effect, in this way making him completely an object of manipulation. But such a deterministic interpretation of identity invites speculation about higher levels of control. The rocket and all the human manipulations surrounding it are subject to the larger physical—and, of course, causal—laws of gravity. The apparent omnipotence of gravity suggests that external forces dictate the course of all events, regardless of what motivations and purposes human beings attribute to their actions.[13] The search for sufficient causes leads to the search for further and more sufficient causes, until it seems that all events are about to link up in an inflexible chain, each action precipitating the next. The world totters on the brink of total intelligibility and coherence. Its history seems about to turn into the track of an inevitable progression of physical forces. Freedom seems about to be exposed as an illusion.

Yet causal explanations do not offer the only way to connect the matter of experience. As the statistician Roger Mexico tells the Pavlovian Dr. Pointsman in *Gravity's Rainbow*, " 'there's a feeling about that cause-and-effect may have been taken as far as it will go. That for science to carry on at all, it must look for a less narrow, less...sterile set of assumptions. The next great breakthrough may come when we have the courage to junk cause-and-effect entirely, and strike off at some other angle' " (p. 89; Pynchon's ellipsis). Furthermore, causal explanations are sanctioned only by the authority of the human beings who, ironically, chose them: shortly after the end of World War II, Albert Einstein wrote, "The growth of our factual knowledge, together with the striving for a unified theoretical conception comprising all empirical data, has led to the present situation which is characterized—nothwithstanding all successes—by an uncertainty concerning the choice of basic theoretical concepts."[14] Einstein's use of the word *choice* here to describe the selection from among possible underpinnings for "a unified theoretical conception comprising all empirical data" suggests that the more inclusive an explanatory structure becomes, the more arbitrary its ground assumptions appear. Relativity theory developed because Newtonian physics, based on the theoretical concept of the determining cause, could not explain, or even admit the possibility of, the "surprises" that Pynchon alludes to in his formulation of Murphy's law: "*when everything has been taken care of, when nothing can go wrong, or even surprise us...something will*" (*GR*, p. 275; Pynchon's ellipsis). A scientific explanation that can survive Murphy's law will not attempt to "take care of" things in so inflexible a fashion.

Pynchon sketches a more flexible kind of explanation in *Gravity's Rainbow* when Leni Pökler insists to her technician husband that causal relations do not exhaust the connections in the universe: " 'Not produce . . . not cause. It all goes along together. Parallel, not series. Metaphor. Signs and symptoms. Mapping on to different coordinate systems . . .' " (p. 159). Such analogical relations have become increasingly important to twentieth-century mathematics and science; in particular, "mapping on to different coordinate systems" is the method by which Gödel constructed the proof of the theorem bearing his name;[15] and in *Gravity's Rainbow*, Gödel's theorem is identified with Murphy's law, the guarantor of "surprises" (p. 275). Furthermore, analogical relations are essential to Pynchon's own narrative strategy. If the traditional novel depends on the familiar links of antecedent and consequent, cause and effect, for its unity, Leni's emphasis on an overall system of formal relations—"Parallel, not series. Metaphor. Signs and symptoms"—calls attention to the importance of resemblance as a structural principle in Pynchon's novels and in the worlds of these novels.

Of course, the one rhetorical figure in Leni's groping catalogue, metaphor, discovers relations of resemblance. A metaphor exposing an unfamiliar, unsuspected resemblance produces "surprises," and the more apparently heterogeneous the ideas that are yoked together, the more surprising the effect. As their affinities with "surprises" might indicate, relations of resemblance, unlike causal relations, are neither determining nor exhaustive. They tend to open doors rather than to close them, as in the string of metaphorical predications implicit in *Gravity's Rainbow*, where the rocket is a phallus, is a thrusting middle finger, is an index finger pointing to ultimate meaning, is a pencil inscribing meaning, is Time's Arrow (in thermodynamic theory), is Zeno's arrow (in several of the paradoxes), and so on, in endlessly receding vistas. And relations of resemblance are frequently used as ordering principles in non-naturalistic novels, where events parallel one another, exposing latent similarities, rather than following one another in successive "slices" from a time-line: clearly Leni's speech constitutes a fair description of Pynchon's narrative strategy in *Gravity's Rainbow*.

But Leni is also insisting that such relations are real proper-
ties of her world, not patterns her artistic sensibility has imposed. We are accustomed to thinking of causal relations as
the true ones, of metaphoric relations as poetic, emotional,
finally subjective. In a world constituted by the "endlessly
diddling play" of language, however, the articulations of the
real are the distinctions and jointures established by language
as it cuts out and assembles a reality for the understanding. In
such a world, rhetorical relations are the real ones, and causality loses its preeminence and becomes another trope: perhaps,
as David Lodge has suggested, a species of metonymy.[16] And
in a world made of language, it is futile to penetrate relations
of resemblance in search of an "underlying" causality.[17]

In *V.*, for example, the women Victoria Wren, Vera
Meroving, Veronica Manganese, and so on clearly have a
great deal in common, including an ominously shared initial.
The metaphoric relation is so pronounced and so intrusive that
it appears to veil stronger, or at any rate more familiar, connections, although *V.* contains no unambiguous statement that
these names signal successive appearances of the same
woman. In this way Pynchon is able to insinuate that the
"real" connection is sequential; that is, that the same V.
makes a series of appearances on the time-line of twentieth-
century history. History thus perceived becomes a developing
plot, whose stages are marked by the "impersonations" of the
increasingly inanimate lady V.

But for all its implications of a cosmic "plot," *V.* itself is not
conventionally plotted. It repeatedly sabotages attempts to
make the action add up, most obviously by juxtaposing chapters that take place in the narrative present and chapters that
take place in a quasi-historical "past." This "past" is not
merely an earlier segment of the same historical continuum. It
is radically different from the present because it exists as a
collection of discrete stories, each having a distinct narrator,
structure, style, and tone. Much of the present action revolves
around Herbert Stencil's efforts to construct a narrative in
which this "past" stands as antecedent to, and cause of, the

present, and thus explains *why* mid-twentieth-century society is apathetic, dehumanized, and liable to erupt into violence. But Stencil's projected plot fails to assimilate all the diverse elements of the book, and thus fails to establish that the world has gone into apocalyptic decline.

In hypothesizing that his culture is a decadence, in the Last Days of its descent toward entropic dissolution, Stencil attributes the torpor and lack of concern that he recognizes in himself and in the people surrounding him to an omnipotent force shaping history. All he can learn, he concludes, is that he can do nothing—either that, or that there is nothing to learn. The irony is that "past" actions and present actions tend to duplicate one another; the juxtaposition of chapters emphasizes their resemblances. Stencil wants to reassemble a fragmented history on a time-line in order to trace a continuous decline, but the various segments of the "past" are also decadent, as full of violence and intellectual inertia as the narrative present. In overlooking the intrusive resemblances between "past" and present in order to resolve everything into a cumulative plot, Stencil ignores exactly the significance that history offers in *V.* In this novel, relations of resemblance yield lessons that the characters, wrapped up in plotting, ignore. *V.* is built on these resemblances: it does not add up, but it does mean.

The Crying of Lot 49 is the most traditional of Pynchon's novels, chronicling the quest of a single central character and reporting on her consecutive discoveries through the mediation of a single omniscient narrator. Early in the story, Oedipa comes across the enigmatic word *Tristero*. The rest of the book details her subsequent encounters with this name, with an associated symbol of a muted post horn, and with the acronym W.A.S.T.E. These signs, Oedipa hopes, will lead to a "real Tristero," an organization hiding behind the visible order. Her search is thus for the cause or source of the signs she has observed among the impoverished and overlooked segments of American society.

But the anticipated conclusion, the unveiling of the Tristero,

never arrives. In the absence of a last word—a "crying"—
Oedipa is left unsure what to make of her accumulated information, unsure whether the outcast, dispossessed population
she has uncovered will be granted importance by virtue of
their place in an enveloping Tristero-system or whether they
will be reduced to absurdity, as discarded "bits" from the
computer-like American system. As the novel ends, she is
waiting to find out. But her dilemma, despite its superficial
persuasiveness, does not reflect the emphasis of the discourse. The Tristero hypothesis has directed Oedipa to a cultural underground, and this has been its significance. The
"wasted" people that Oedipa has come to recognize are important not because they participate in a larger and implicitly
redemptive organization presided over by an outside power,
but because they do not participate in the American system;
they are indices that the American system has failed. The
sleight-of-hand that makes the main action of the novel a quest
for the cause of the signs is a trick of misdirection. The name
"Tristero," the post horn, and the acronym are pointers, calling attention to an alienated subculture, a group of isolates
who paradoxically have isolation in common.

In *Gravity's Rainbow* Pynchon takes the rigidity of causal
relations a step further, making such relations the necessarily
incomplete perceptions of a time-bound humanity viewing an
eternal structure. The arc of the V-2 rocket, the "gravity's
rainbow" of the title, functions as a sort of visual aid to conceiving history as a preordained curve with a clearly demarcated beginning, middle, and end.

But this totalizing metaphor does not contain the action of
the book, for the action continues to burgeon in unanticipated
directions, revealing new resemblances in the process until it
seems that things cannot add up to a coherent whole *because*
they are so intricately interrelated. Furthermore, the protean
narrator serves as a reminder that there is no privileged outside perspective commanding a view of "the whole shape at
once." The world exists as an indefinite number of partial,

contingent, and overlapping versions; and by shifting points of view, often with unnerving rapidity, this narrator multiplies angles and opens up new vistas of possibility. He often borrows idiosyncratic personal mannerisms, cultural biases, and habits of thought from characters ("Fine crew this is, getting set to go after the Radiant—say what? what's Slothrop's *own* gift and Fatal Flaw! Aw *c'mon* . . . "), adopts an elevated tone, particularly in passages of direct address ("But just over the embankment, down in the arena, what might that have been just now, waiting in this broken moonlight, camouflage paint from fins to point crazed into jigsaw . . . is it, then, really never to find you again?"), or lapses into elbow-nudging jocularity ("That is, all over the walls, photograffiti, are pictures of Horrible Disasters in German Naval History. Collisions, magazine explosions, U-boat sinkings, just the thing if you're an officer trying to take a shit"). By diffusing his personae in this way (rather as Slothrop diffuses into multiple manifestations in the last part of the novel), this narrator manages to be authoritative without being omniscient in the conventional sense—which is to say transcendent. Through this narrator Pynchon is able to evoke a world perceived from inside, without suggesting that this point of view is purely personal or subjective and hence untrustworthy. One implication is that all possible perspectives on human life are inside perspectives; experience has no outside except the one that people try to imagine when they postulate some controlling force beyond their understanding.[18] From inside, the universe is full of connections, but no quasi-authorial sanction guarantees that one idea of order is the ultimate one. Experience becomes a layering or moiré of orders, growing more complex and more interconnected with every new perspective, never resolving into a single comprehensible pattern. For all its rhetoric of inevitability, *Gravity's Rainbow* is an open structure, built on the perception of what the narrator at one point calls "Kute Korrespondences," and playing on the impossibility of exhausting the "permutations 'n' combinations" of its narrated elements.

Readers engrossed in the project of getting at Pynchon's Holy Center are forced to minimize this kind of energy and exuberance, a strong indication that the center is missing for a reason. In Pynchon's work humor cannot be written off as a diversionary tactic. The pervasive slanginess of the novels ("—say what? yes lookit inside his GI undershorts here's a sneaky *hardon* stirring, ready to jump"), the puns (Manny diPresso; the Hobbesian law firm of Saltieri, Poore, Nash, DeBrutus, and Short; the elaborately set up spinoff from the maxim about forty million Frenchmen, "For De Mille, young fur-henchmen can't be rowing!"), the parodically "typical" occurrences (Suck Hour at the Sailors' Grave Tavern, the Yoyodyne Board of Directors' Songfest), the whimsical transitions ("You will want cause and effect. All right."), and the implausibly and intrusively named characters (Benny Profane, Stanley Koteks, Webley Silvernail, and so on) are all factors that warp the narrative away from linearity, keep it from proceeding straightforwardly toward its presumed goal.

It is because they succeed in foxing inevitability that the novels are ultimately comic. As I shall argue in greater detail in the chapters that follow, *V.*, *The Crying of Lot 49*, and *Gravity's Rainbow* constantly violate expectation with abrupt shifts in tone, unforeseen plot developments, and contextual implausibilities. Such violations not only deflate incipient high seriousness but provide new frameworks for multiplying possibilities and discerning unimagined correspondences.

2

Duplicity and Duplication in *V.*

It has become a critical commonplace that *V.*, Pynchon's first novel, is directly concerned with the nature and limits of human knowledge. *V.* may be described as an epistemological fable, or fable of knowing, in that it raises questions about what an individual character knows or can know, in order to invoke the larger issue of the conditions and possibilities of knowledge *per se*.[1] As an ironically modified questing hero, Herbert Stencil, one of the novel's two protagonists, is absorbed in connecting the multifarious data of his experience into a revelatory pattern. His goal is to identify V., a project assuming at the outset that V. is the sort of thing that can be identified. But at what should be the climactic moment of his quest, Stencil realizes that he is pinned between two contradictory but equally compelling world views. "Events seem to be ordered into an ominous logic," he finds himself muttering (p. 423), and one of two conclusions seems to follow from this logic. Either the lady V. exists, in which case the Plot Which Has No Name dominates the fictional present, or the lady V. does not exist, and Stencil has hypothesized or even hallucinated relations between random events. In the first case, a repressive order manipulates events; in the second, apparent order veils real chaos. But one irony of this formulation is that neither explanation comprehends the information confronting Stencil. A further irony is that this dilemma has even less application to the information confronting the reader.[2]

The assumptions on which Stencil proceeds are fundamentally naturalistic, in that he approaches his evidence as if it encoded a traditional story line, in this case centering on the adventures of a malevolently picaresque heroine. He works on the supposition that if the incidents of his father's life do not add up to a conventional plot—which takes on overtones of "conspiracy"—they are entirely unconnected, and thus late in the book he comes to suspect that his reconstructed history adds up to nothing more than "the recurrence of an initial and a few dead objects" (p. 419). But even such an admission of failure begs the question, for it does not explain why the initial and the objects recur so intrusively in the history that he studies. Stencil's project of identification runs up against the convention of duplication that is the governing structural principle of *V.*, which is only to say that Stencil's story does not approximate Pynchon's.

Yet Stencil's story is enormously persuasive—as are Stencil's presumptions about what a story is. A "Stencilized" reading of the events in *V.* vacillates between two poles of interpretation that on examination turn out to have exactly the same consequences. Thus, if V. exists, her "plot" is so far-reaching that it effectively makes the contemporary world a closed system, subject to eventual entropic rundown that terminates in a state of chaos. If V. does not exist, her absence effectively guarantees that the world is already chaotic. In essence, the two lines of interpretation converge at a point of chaos, the nadir of a structural V.

In this way Stencil reduplicates the V-symbol and makes incoherence the truth about a fictional world characterized by ballooning implications of coherence. For the V-symbol is chronically overdetermined. It signifies, and thus associates, not only the women that Stencil identifies as successive manifestations of the lady V. (Victoria Wren, Vera Meroving, Veronica Manganese, and so on), but places (Venezuela, Valletta, Vheissu, the V-Note Tavern), qualities (*virtú*, velocity, violence), and even symbols *for* association (V is the logical sign for "or"; > is the logical symbol for implication and the notation for vectors).[3] Theses that the lady V. exists— or that she does not exist, for that matter—do not explain the intrusive presence of the letter V in these diverse contexts, and the intrusive presence of the letter V is the central enigma of the novel.

But the impulse to translate the events of the novel into evidence for or against V.'s existence is difficult to resist because Pynchon's fictional worlds are very evidently overlapping networks of codes. Modernist conventions suggest that readers who break these codes will arrive at a statement about what "really" happens, and *V.* is the most overt of the three novels in inviting criticism of a particular kind, criticism that in its aims and methods is analogous to sleuthing. Yet the invitation to play literary detective is duplicitous. Too many clues turn out to be red herrings.

In fact, there is no way to decode or reassemble this text so that it reads sequentially, yielding definitive information about who V. "really" is or what "really" happened to Stencil's father. But if *V.* does not have a unitary narrative thread, it achieves coherence in other ways, through repetition of key patterns and themes on different levels, through the juxtaposition of incidents in the "real time" of the narrative present and the "mirror time" of the narrative past, and through the recurring initial. The metaphoric duplications are so pervasive that they give the novel a labyrinthine, box-within-box structure: for all its preoccupation with history, *V.* is static and spatial rather than dynamic and progressive. It is the *presence* of the past that signifies, not an obscured chronology that relegates history to nonexistence except as a residual force or influence.

Within this context Stencil's quest acts as a lure, promising an embedded plot that will culminate in a vision of what his story—and, by implication, history—means. By offering the character of Stencil as a critical role model, *V.* duplicitously fosters the epistemological assumption that experience is somehow a story that will yield up its significance when it is given, as Robert Musil's Man without Qualities puts it, "a unidimensional order: the stringing upon one thread of all that has happened in space and time, in short, that notorious 'narrative thread' of which it then turns out the thread of life consists."[4] In the midst of multiple patterns of connectedness, Stencil feverishly sorts, subordinates, and rejects data like a chronologizing Maxwell's Demon, committed to the proposition that events must be strung on that notorious narrative thread if they are to have any order at all. His vision of history is teleological: either incidents add up to something or they are wholly meaningless. And so his quest becomes a selective misreading of the novel, based on a particular, limited understanding of what constitutes a meaningful pattern.

This misreading is part of the humor of *V.*, but it has its darker side. Stencil's avowed aim is both to bring history to a close by finding V. and to avoid such closure because it implicates him. A plot, after all, is a completed action; and once Stencil decides that the twentieth century must be plotted to have any form at all, he is committed to the assumption that he will be able to understand this history only when it has ended. This recognition forces him into a kind of agnosticism. His motto is "approach and avoid," and his task, like the traditional fiction writer's, is to keep the space of narrative action open so he can maintain the illusion that the "middle" realm of history that he inhabits has not already collapsed into its terminus. His enterprise grows increasingly desperate as he realizes its magnitude. But this enterprise also grows increasingly estranged from the action of the novel. If Stencil fails to assimilate the events around him to his grandiose schema, this does not indicate that these events have no meaning. It indicates, rather, that meaning is not the exclusive property of narrative resolutions. *V.* is a novel that does not add up, but does mean. And in presenting Stencil as a bogus exemplum, it underscores the danger of granting significance to experience only when that experience is perceived *sub specie resolutionis*.

V.'s six "past" chapters (including the epilogue) reflect and comment on events in the "present" narrative, but they cannot be naturalized to the point where they are simply antecedent to the present: the reader never discovers what Stencil is searching for, the *cause* of mid-twentieth-century decadence, apathy, and violence. Yet the static effect of the metaphoric structure, which suggests that past and present exist simultaneously or even that they are reversible, places the emphasis on analogical rather than serial relationships. The ability to recognize analogical relationships is the ability to learn from past experiences. But in *V.*, where past and present reflect each other in receding vistas, nobody seems to learn anything. Benny Profane's last words in the book are "Offhand I'd say I haven't learned a goddamn thing" (p. 428), and this remark sums up the experience of all the major characters. The great irony of Stencil's characterization is not that he perceives connections where none exist but that he continually searches for the wrong kinds of connections while ignoring the metaphorical relations that are staring him in the face.

Throughout *V.* Stencil remains oblivious to the resemblances between the facts that he unearths and the actions taking place around him. The past for him is a cipher, and if it yields to his zealous decoding, it can only reveal the reason why things cannot be otherwise than they are. In searching for V., he is after "The Big One, the century's master cabal" (p. 210), origin of the "plot" of his own story and thus of modern history.[5] Because he posits a developing "plot" that has him in its clutches, he ignores the ways in which history repeats itself and remains unaware that his own actions mimic an earlier pattern. In making V. "a historical fact [who] continued active today" (p. 210), he tries to establish a link between himself and his dead father. But the most important connection between the Stencils *père* and *fils* is a shared tendency to construe order as conspiracy and to "read" information as if it veiled or disguised a single malevolent intention.

In a sense both Stencils are consummate novel-readers, so inured to fictional conventions of a certain sort that they can anticipate the machinations of a hidden author and predict the reversal in which apparently insignificant or unrelated details will be revealed as necessary to the resolution. Because they are implicated in the story, they are especially sensitive to the punning significance of "plot" and see the force manipulating them as hostile. The inevitable recognition, which will bestow retrospective significance on prior events and show how these events constituted a chain of causes leading up to the climax, will only affirm that they are in someones else's power and that they have helped bring the story to its destined conclusion. Yet precisely because the Stencils are adept at reading formulaic, "stenciled" texts, they are incapable of reading a novel by Pynchon. They assume that the important ordering principles will be identity and causality, and so they miss the multiplying resemblances and the governing convention of doubling.

Ironically, this peculiarly Stencilian myopia is itself doubled in *V*. In his quest to complete his father's narrative and reveal the "real" story, Herbert Stencil assumes that things are related only if they have a single trait or property in common. In particular, he is obsessed with disclosing an unbroken narrative thread lying beneath the disparate incidents of his own life and the life of his father. For this reason he remains blind to a very literal instance of what Wittgenstein (who is quoted in *V*.) has called family resemblances: relations based on "a complicated network of similarities, overlapping and criss-crossed: sometimes overlapping similarities, sometimes similarities of detail."[6] He fails to see that his intuition of a cosmic plot lurking under the appearance of diversity echoes his father's predilection for interpreting experience in terms of alias, disguise, and code. Yet one of the most obvious connections between the two Stencils is that their habits of mind are very similar. In their inability to recognize family resemblances, the Stencils have a marked family resemblance.

The "stenciled" reading of experience looks for the central

and climactic truth veiled by a variegated surface of appearances, but the structure of *V.* seems more a matter of family resemblances. For example, in chapter seven, "She hangs on the western wall," the initial V. calls attention to links between Botticelli's rendering of Venus, the Gaucho's adopted homeland of Venezuela, the girl Victoria Wren, Machiavellian *virtú*, Hugh Godolphin's barbarous land of Vheissu, and the volcanic mountain Vesuvius. None of these V-words sums up or holds the key to the entire story, but each sets up a range of resonances establishing connections with other V-words on several levels—through references to *The Prince*, the Bible, classical mythology, and art history; through metaphor, as in the sexual, social, and geological connotations of "eruption"; and through overlapping strands of plot. Like all the "past" chapters, "She hangs on the western wall" is a tour de force of narrative technique, in this case of a style of omniscient narration that manages to balance the concerns of six main characters without giving precedence to any one of them. Just as no one V-word encapsulates the significance of the letter V in this chapter, no one character emerges as central, and no one action achieves prominence, subsuming the other actions to a grand design. The plot of this chapter remains multiple, involving four separate actions intertwined by a network of local and contingent relations. Sidney Stencil's attempt to translate a complex of these relations into a cohesive sinister Situation that subordinates diverse events to a governing intention is only one of these actions.

Within this context of irreducibly multiple concerns, the elder Stencil labors to realize his ideal of narrative coherence. His assumption that the various V-words conceal or encode an identity leads him into a quest after the "real" meaning of Vheissu, an exotically remote country whose name, like the initial V., fuctions as a free-floating signifier. Vheissu refuses to yield up a fundamental referent under his probing. Instead, it accretes other V words—"Venezuela," "Vesuvius," "volcano"—and as Stencil struggles to synthesize all of them, he is driven to construct an increasingly comprehensive plot which finally postulates that agents of an unknown power plan to infiltrate and conquer Western civilization. The fantasy swells to global proportions precisely because "Vheissu" is neither a cover nor an alias: as Hugh Godolphin confides to Signor Mantissa, the secret of Vheissu is that it hides Nothing beneath its particolored skin—a message that Stencil misses, at least in part because his promotion of his own theory drives Godolphin out of Florence. If "Vheissu" encodes anything, it is a pun—"Wie heisst du?," "What is your name?"[7]—that parodies Stencil's preoccupation with *sub rosa* identities.

The younger Stencil inherits this preoccupation. The impetus for his quest comes from an entry in his father's journal, "There is more behind and inside V. than any of us had suspected. Not who, but what: what is she. God grant that I may never be called upon to write the answer, either here or in any official report" (p. 43). Herbert Stencil's initial piece of detective work is to decode this passage in a way that delimits V. and gives him some purchase on the elusive signifier his father has thrown into question. He accordingly tries to define V. so that she has global and even cosmic implications but still remains the kind of being he can reasonably expect to find. Although she has enormous symbolic weight—she is the key to "The Big One, the century's master cabal" (p. 210)—she must also be a person: "A woman," as an early confidante suggests. That is, her various manifestations must be appropriate to a character in a naturalistic fiction. She cannot be in two places at the same time, for instance, and her character must be explicable in terms of her prior experiences and proclivities. "Disguise is one of her attributes," Stencil assures Benny Profane (p. 363); and V.'s capacity for disguise helps him justify his theory that Victoria Wren, who put on a "young, crude Mata Hari act in Egypt" before she moved to Florence, is the same woman who turns up in Southwest Africa in 1913 under the name of Vera Meroving, and in Malta during the 1944 siege as the Bad Priest.

In essence, Stencil's preconceptions about what a story is

prompt him to put arbitrary limits on V. Starting with an initial, Stencil tries to build a metonymic narrative out of patterns of recurrence. Like his prototype Henry Adams, he finds the woman "easiest to handle,"[8] and so the story purporting to make sense of "the recurrence of an initial and a few dead objects" becomes a series of adventures linking his heroine with a selection of twentieth-century catastrophes. But his story cannot encompass all manifestations of the V symbol, even though he frequently qualifies his assumptions about V.'s identity in an attempt to assimilate new implications. When he finally makes his decision to go to Malta, the narrator of the "present" chapters deadpans, "V. by this time was a remarkably scattered concept" (p. 364). And most of the appearances of the V symbol remain scattered outside the narrative framework that Stencil tries to build around them.

Despite Stencil's efforts to keep V. within conventional boundaries of character, she continually emerges in forms that the terms of the quest cannot account for. From Stencil's standpoint, "To go along assuming that Victoria the girl tourist and Veronica the sewer rat were one and the same V. was not at all to bring up any metempsychosis . . . " (p. 210); but his theory of disguise will not explain how Veronica, who is indubitably a rat, albeit a beatified rat, and Victoria, the girl tourist at Fashoda, can be "one and the same V." And regardless of whether the lady V. does or does not exist, the various V-words that constitute Stencil's clues are simply there. The thesis that V. is a historical personage does not account for the recurrence of the V-symbol in words like "Venus," "Vesuvius," "Venezuela," and "*virtú*." Still less does this thesis account for manifestations of the V-symbol that turn up in the fictional present: Valletta, velocity, the V-Note Tavern and its competitor the Forked Yew (whose patrons, updating *Lear*, are the twentieth century's poor "forked" creatures), and the Vs of migratory birds, intersecting streets, and spread thighs. The Vs proliferate beyond Stencil's quasi-authorial control, so that though Stencil defines himself as He Who

Looks for V., it is the reader who keeps running into her—or it.

By "plotting" a curve through various appearances of the initial, Stencil in effect constructs a myth of origins. His thesis that manifestations of the V-symbol add up to a quasi-allegorical figure who acts as the presiding genius of a socially entropic, terminally ill century is an attempt to account for the mid-fifties culture of the novel's "present" sections. This culture is for the most part dehumanized, half-conscious, and absorbed in banal fetishes; the narrator repeatedly calls it a decadence. But by making these tendencies into a global movement and giving this movement a name and a genesis, Stencil endows a selection of events with the shape of necessity. By constructing a plot to explain how a process of reification began, he commits this process to a determinate end.

Stencil is only concerned to amass evidence proving that his epoch's descent into the inanimate is proceeding as planned. For this reason it is important that Stencil's reading of the evidence does not embrace all the manifestations of the V-symbol. His projected plot translates contemporary history into apocalypse and makes individual choice either impossible or irrelevant. But Stencil's failure to link the V-word coherently does not indicate that Stencil has merely fantasized or hallucinated a relation between a random collection of terms. For among other things *V.* does contain a sort of story about a sort of eponymous heroine. Chapter three, "In which Stencil, a quick-change artist, does eight impersonations," deals with an espionage murder in Alexandria on the eve of the Fashoda Incident and includes the young Victoria Wren among its characters. Chapter seven, "She hangs on the western wall," associates Victoria with the Situation in Florence at the turn of the century and gives her her first piece of characteristic hardware, a comb carved in the shape of a multiple crucifixion. Chapter nine, "Mondaugen's story," takes place in 1922 in the German Southwest Protectorate, and brings back Hugh Godolphin and a woman named Vera Meroving, who claims to know Godolphin from Florence and who has a clockwork eye. Chapter eleven, "Confessions of Fausto Maijstral," includes Maijstral's eyewitness report of the 1944 dismantling of the Bad Priest, who proves to be a woman and who has the comb, the clockwork eye, artificial feet, and a star sapphire sewn into her navel. Chapter fourteen, "V. in love," is set in Paris in 1913 and revolves around the fetishistic love affair between a lady called only V. and a young ballerina. The epilogue, set in Malta in 1919, deals with the last days of Sidney Stencil and puts him in the company of Veronica Manganese, who recalls their affair in Florence, an affair that might have made her the mother of Herbert Stencil. Manganese wears the comb and the glass eye and wishes for artificial feet; Stencil remembers the star sapphire sewn in her navel.

The initial V., the recurring combinations of the "few dead objects," and some bits of dialogue or narrative asides appear to guarantee that "one and the same V." appears in each of these chapters. What is interesting, however, is that this V.'s presence is the *only* conventional narrative link between all the "past" chapters. Sidney Stencil, Hugh Godolphin, and Evan Godolphin each appear in two, and Stencil is mentioned in a third; but in general each chapter introduces a new cast of characters. Furthermore, the lady V. plays very different roles in the different stories and gets very different kinds of narrative treatment. In fact, the "past" chapters are so inescapably different from one another—and from the "present" chapters—that they raise the problem of V.'s identity to another level, and on this level the reader becomes implicated in the premises of Stencil's quest.

Each of the "past" chapters is a completed action; each, with the possible exception of the epilogue, could be detached from the novel and read as a short story.[9] The implied continuity between these distinct segments of V.'s history is based more on resemblance that on temporal sequence: each story associates the lady V. with some version of a documented historical incident, and in each case the incident is violent (another V). Furthermore, the sequence is deliberately fragmented in two ways. First, the "past" chapters are not grouped together but placed at irregular intervals between the "present" chapters, so that they offer an ironic counterpoint to the action set in the narrative present. Second, these chapters do not occur in chronological order and consequently do not chronicle the continuous development of the lady V., or of the "plot" to which she seems to have some undefined relation.

It is perfectly possible to reconstruct a partial biography of V. from these chapters, and a number of critics have done so. However, this kind of reassembly raises more problems than it solves. In the first place, V. emerges as a parody of character development. She "grows" by a literal processes of accretion, assimilating inanimate objects into her body with the passage of time until at her death she is simply decomposed—again, quite literally. This mechanical rendering of development denies any insight into V.'s motives and intentions and fails to elucidate her relation to the outbreaks of violence her presence seems to signal. She always seems more a symbol than a character, calling attention to such repeated motifs as decadence, the inanimate, and the polarized visions of "hothouse" and "Street," paired terms reflecting the pseudo-dilemma of a rigidly "plotted" order versus total chaos. Reconstructing V. in this way only emphasizes the multiple levels on which V. herself is a construction.

Second, this reconstructed "plot" does not add up to any climactic revelation. It appears that V. lived and died—died eleven years before the action of the "present" narrative begins. There is a hint in the epilogue that she is Herbert Stencil's mother, but the information is extremely equivocal: in the long run, it reveals only that Victoria Wren seduced the elder Stencil in the year preceding Herbert Stencil's birth. This obscure clue suggests a causal link between past and present, but it remains only a clue. There is no detective-story dénouement in which it is either affirmed or denied. Stencil's own thesis is that the revelation is still to come, but to maintain this thesis, he must presume that the lady V. is alive and well: "If she was a historical fact then she continued active today and at the moment, because the ultimate Plot Which Has No Name was as yet unrealized . . . " (p. 210). For this reason he has to reject certain pieces of evidence, notably Maijstral's story of the death of the Bad Priest. Yet this story seems to guarantee that V. is dead, at least if the "Confessions of Fausto Maijstral" can be trusted.

The third and most serious problem with reconstructing the history of V., however, is that the text raises unanswerable questions about which of the "past" narrators is trustworthy. The reader can string "past" chapters on a story line to produce a fundamentally naturalistic narrative only by ignoring the naturalistic question of where these chapters come from. But *V.* persists in raising this question in complex and confusing ways.

The eleven "present" chapters describe the adventures of Benny Profane, Herbert Stencil, the Whole Sick Crew, and various associates and hangers-on during the years 1955 and 1956. These chapters seem relatively straightforward because they respect what David Lodge has called metonymic standards of coherence: they adhere to chronological sequence and have a single omniscient narrator.[10] But the "present" action also refuses to add up. Herbert Stencil looks for V. but does not find her. Various young people get together and then drift apart. Major and minor characters remain absorbed in the ostentatiously trivial activities that absorbed them when they first appeared. The structural metaphor for the "present" seems to be Profane's habit of yo-yoing, and the well-intentioned (*bene*) Benny himself, the presiding deity of a profane world, travels in a circumscribed orbit that is finally a parody of the linear plot, going from Norfolk to New York to Valletta without learning anything.

Because the structure of the "present" chapters emphasizes the failure of learning, the "past" chapters that mysteriously punctuate the dominant story line acquire additional emphasis. The significance of the "present" action somehow resides in these self-contained stories, each having a different kind of construction and narrative mode. "In which Stencil . . . " begins with a short prologue in the narrative present and then switches abruptly to an Alexandria reminiscent of Durrell. The ensuing story falls into eight sections, the first seven narrated from the point of view of some minor character and the eighth using an omniscient narrator. "She hangs on the western wall" begins with another such prologue and then shifts to the Florence setting and an omniscient narrator who moves in and out of the minds of the six main characters but does not step back to comment on the significance or morality of the action. If the bumbling espionage in this chapter recalls *Our Man in Havana*, the Vheissu passages overtly parody *Heart of Darkness*. "Mondaugen's story" has a third person narrator who takes Mondaugen's point of view while maintaining some distance from the character and offering introductory remarks on his psychology. This narrator is the most conspicuously amoral, describing what are probably the most repellent incidents of the novel from a stance of nail-pairing detachment. The "Confessions of Fausto Maijstral" is a first-person narration by one of the "present" characters who uses the confessional mode with a self-consciously Augustinian awareness of temporality and a self-consciously Proustian sense of the gap between the writer and his "rejected personalities." "V. in love" has an omniscient narrator who is extremely detached from the action and who makes lengthy, sententious pronouncements from the vantage of tolerant, slightly weary wisdom. The diction and syntax of this chapter are excessively stilted; combined with the Parisian setting and the Balzacian tone, they suggest that the story has been translated too literally from the French. The epilogue is a third-person narration entering only the consciousness of Sidney Stencil, although the closing paragraph, which suddenly addresses the reader, seems to grant this narrator omniscience. The manifest differences between these chapters, especially the differences in narrative voice, all but preclude any possibility of reassembling a "real" story. Taken together, the "past" chapters appear to provide different perspectives on different incidents, so that stringing them on a time-line raises the major question of the reliable narrator.

What finally makes such a process of reassembly even more inappropriate is that four of these six "past" chapters are linked to the "present" narrative by hints that their third-person narrators are "really" a first-person narrator incognito. The prologues to "In which Stencil . . . " and "She hangs on the western wall" and information in the chapters preceding "Mondaugen's story" and "V. in love" imply—although never unambiguously—that the stories are there because Stencil tells them. If this is the case, there is no way to distinguish fact from Stencilian fiction, an implication that the text reinforces in numerous ways. For example, the title of "In which Stencil . . . " intimates that the eight narrators of the consecutive segments are Stencil's own "impersonations." In the prologue to "She hangs on the western wall," the "soul-dentist" Eigenvalue reflects, "Yet we have men like Stencil, who must go about grouping the world's random caries into cabals" (p. 139), suggesting that the evidence for V. amounts to a concatenation of purely accidental details. The chapter preceding "Mondaugen's story" appears to give an account of that story's origins: "The tale proper and the questioning after took no more than thirty minutes. Yet the next Wednesday afternoon at Eigenvalue's office, when Stencil retold it, the yarn had undergone considerable change: had become, as Eigenvalue put it, Stencilized" (p. 211). "So what year is it," says Profane at the close of chapter thirteen. "It is 1913," Stencil replies (p. 368), and the opening paragraph of the following chapter, "V. in love," confirms that "it is" indeed 1913, in Paris. True to his name, Stencil seems to be stenciling the figures of his obsession all over his father's personal landscape, and it would follow that four of the six "past" chapters are "really" imaginative reconstructions.

But just as the text sabotages the naturalistic project of

reconstructing the "past" chapters to get at the "real" story of the lady V., it also sabotages the naturalistic project of writing off these chapters as fabrications and thus aspects of Stencil's psychology rather than components of the plot. To reconstruct the "past" chapters in a linear sequence without regard to their different points of view is to embrace Stencil's assumption that disparate events always decode as aspects of a single conspiracy. The irony of this kind of reconstruction is that so very little comes of it: the conspiracy is not laid bare when V.'s life is reassembled. But to deny these "past" chapters any "real" status within the narrative is also to embrace a Stencilian assumption, for the reader who decodes these chapters as Stencil's disguises and impersonations duplicates Stencil's attempts to decode appearances of the V symbol as manifestations of "one and the same V." And this approach also fails to yield a satisfactory reading of the novel, for a number of reasons.

Most obviously, this thesis only accounts for four of the six "past" chapters. Nothing in the "Confessions of Fausto Maijstral" indicates that its author might have made up or hallucinated the episode of the Bad Priest's death, and the Bad Priest collects in her own person all the "dead objects" that have served as clues to V.'s continuing identity; in fact, she is what all these clues add up to. As a culminating synthesis, she is something of an anticlimax; but at the moment of anti-climax, when the children take her apart, she also validates several aspects of the other "past" chapters that make V. a single, continuing character.

The epilogue is even more problematic. There are no framing devices around this final section; nothing even hints that its narrator is "really" a character. As a consequence, this chapter simply stands, without being located in any way within the "present" narrative. Its narrator claims the same authority as the narrator of the "present" sections, and the text offers nothing to discredit this authority. Although it cannot be naturalized to the context of the "present" chapters, it seems equally "real," and its presumed reality also validates a number of details in the other "past" chapters. The effect of the epilogue is to blur the distinction between "real" and "imagined" information beyond recovery. But in *V.* this distinction is meaningless in any case. The theory that Stencil is the author of four of the six "past" chapters does not explain anything.

For there is no way to make sense of either Stencil's motives or his capacities for inventing four of the most impressive chapters in the novel without allowing his character to balloon to such dimensions that he loses his defining features. It is credible that his monomania drives him to make up stories ambiguously related to a "real" past, but monomania does not account for the stories Stencil is supposed to tell or the manner in which he tells them. For example, Mondaugen's dream, which seems a "forcible dislocation" of Mondaugen's own personality, has little direct relevance to Stencil's quest for V. Yet this dream, the meticulously documented[11] account of how a young German soldier discovers the "operational sympathy" between murderer and victim, is the climax of "Mondaugen's story." No narrative commentary integrates it with V.'s activities or even explains where it comes from. It simply stands, a nostalgic paean to a kind of decadence that history has replaced with another kind of decadence, culminating in a brilliant cumulative sentence well over a page in length (pp. 254–55). If Stencil has given "Mondaugen's story" its structure, it is puzzling that this structure builds to an incident having no direct relevance to his stated concerns. It is possible, of course, to invent explanations for this anomaly. Perhaps Stencil's primary concerns are artistic, so that his commitment to negative capability overrides his ostensible commitment to the quest. Perhaps Stencil's identity is so precarious that he invariably loses himself in his reconstructions. Perhaps as an author Stencil transcends his characteristic limitations and becomes capable of seeing metaphoric and thematic connections that are more important than the metonymic connections giving the lady V. a genesis and a history. But such conjectures expand the boundaries of the character so much that Stencil threatens to become as ubiquitous as V. We accept Stencil the author at the expense of Stencil the character.

In the long run, the theory that swells the limited, myopic Stencil into a virtual persona of the author does little to make sense of a narrative that jumps intermittently into a nostalgia-laden past, and jumps on two occasions without Stencil's help. The "past" chapters do not depend on this connection for their importance. Like the sewer stories of Profane's sojourn under the streets of New York, "they just are. Truth or falsity don't apply" (p. 108). But their positions in the novel magnify the implications of repeated motifs and themes. What is important, finally, is that these motifs and themes are duplicated on all sorts of levels and with all sorts of variations.

For if history is not a cabal in *V.*, this fact does not condemn it to incoherence—to the status of "random caries," as Eigenvalue puts it. History does have a pattern in this book; it is organized by a sort of repetition compulsion that rages unchecked because no one seems to see it. In "Mondaugen's story," for instance, there is an interesting break in tone when the hitherto dispassionate narrator, describing von Trotha's extermination campaign against the Hereros, adds, "Allowing for natural causes during these unnatural years, von Trotha, who stayed for only one of them, is reckoned to have done away with about 60,000 people. This is only 1 per cent of six million, but still pretty good" (p. 227). The unexpectedly flip sarcasm of this remark (the only one of its kind in the chapter) emphasizes a vertical perspective on the subsequent events of Foppl's seige party. Outside Foppl's villa German soldiers gun down a straggling remnant of the Herero tribe that has somehow survived the carnage of fifteen years earlier. Inside, Foppl's guests act out their nostalgia for the genocide of 1904–7 in an orgy of violence that turns into unabashed death-worship. The characters Mondaugen and Weissmann serve to suggest how the same scenario will be transposed into the context of the Third Reich.[12] In addition, the "present" chapters framing the story duplicate its motifs on other levels, as in Mafia Winsome's intellectual racism[13] or the self-conscious decadence of the Whole Sick Crew.

The pattern of duplication is horrifying. But the narrative comment that calls attention to it also calls attention to the disparate human agents who are responsible for genocide. By suggesting that von Trotha was in competition with Hitler, the narrator implicitly denies that an irreversible force produced both of them. Historical episodes resemble each other, but this resemblance does not signal an underlying "plot." Even decadence is a recurring phenomenon in *V.*, although characters always view it apocalyptically as the running-down of history.[14] The important thing about resemblances is that they can be recognized; it is always possible, if highly unlikely in Pynchon's view, that someone will learn.

That the novel encourages conventional and "stenciled" expectations only to undermine them is consequently to the point. Since the Romantics, writers have been fascinated by the *topos* of art as the painted veil over the abyss, the pattern obscuring the void, or, as Hugh Godolphin sees it, the tattooed skin that conceals Nothing. But this version of underlying chaos is thoroughly hyperbolic because it denies the name of order to any state of affairs short of a comprehensive "plot" like the one once attributed to Providence. It locates significance "underneath" experience and refuses to acknowledge that the relations among events, objects, and people constitute local patterns and yield local meanings. It fails to recognize that there are different kinds of relations than those pointing to a controlling designer who manipulates history to a preordained conclusion. Taken to its extreme, as it is in *V.*, this constricted vocabulary of order and chaos makes action pointless and learning impossible.

As a fable of knowing, *V.* seems calculated to provoke a recognition of how impoverished this vocabulary of order and chaos is. In *The Crying of Lot 49*, when Oedipa confronts the same binary alternatives, the narrator comments, "She had heard all about excluded middles; they were bad shit, to be avoided; and how had it ever happened here, with the chances once so good for diversity?" (p. 136). The question is not which alternative describes the "real" state of affairs, or even which alternative is preferable, but how the options got so limited. In *V.* it is the reader who is tempted to reconstruct the "ominous logic" of the novel's world, and the irony is that this "ominous logic" is not even good logic: the two poles of cosmic "plot" and total randomness leave room for any number of "middles." This pseudo-dilemma does not exhaust the possibilities. The novel itself is not constructed according to either of them. The encouragement that *V.* offers to such reconstructions is duplicitous, for *V.* evades reduction through its structural dependence on proliferating duplications: recurring character types, repeated circumstances, reflected themes, and a reiterated initial. Ultimately, this evasion of reduction is consistent with the real subject of *V.* By using a metaphoric structure instead of a conventional plot—by placing the emphasis on resemblances rather than on chronological development—Pynchon could take the twentieth century as his subject in *V.* and write of its devastations without committing it to a fixed and final destiny.

3

Purity as Parody in *The Crying of Lot 49*

In many ways *The Crying of Lot 49* seems to respond to those reviewers who maintained that in *V.* Pynchon was unable to control his subject matter.[1] If nothing else, *Lot 49* is a controlled novel. On the surface, at least, it is a minimalist remake of *V.*, with the disconcerting side trips, flashbacks, and duplications pared away to expose the order/chaos dichotomy in its pristine horror. But the two novels are not variations on the same theme, with *V.* a more circuitous version of *Lot 49*. In *V.* order and chaos emerge as equally untenable interpretive categories, and the joke is that neither can contain and explain the proliferating manifestations of the V symbol. In *Lot 49*, despite the heightened parody, the joke is far less evident. Order and chaos make a more credible claim to be the only possible interpretations of a straightforwardly narrated action that continually strains toward closure. The problem in *Lot 49* is not that order and chaos are inadequate encapsulations of the world of Oedipa Maas; the problem is that both order and chaos are interpretations that could comprehend this world completely—reducing it in the process to inconsequence.

It is the apparent straightforwardness of *Lot 49*'s narration that makes it appear especially vulnerable to definitive interpretation. Whereas both *V.* and *Gravity's Rainbow* have multiple narrators and a disjointed chronology, *The Crying of Lot 49* has an omniscient narrator who follows the single main character, Oedipa Maas, through a series of adventures, each building on the last. These two factors, the stable point of view and the chronological sequence of the narration, distinguish *Lot 49* from the other two novels and make it seem more familiar and intelligible in its premises. Everything is oriented toward Oedipa's discovery of her "legacy," her revelatory Grail. There is less sense of trickery in this novel than in the other two: less sense that events constitute pieces of a gigantic puzzle passed on to the reader for reassembly.[2]

I want to argue, however, that this structural purity is finally parodic. In the process of producing an exemplary linear narrative, Pynchon has in effect written a commentary on the conventions governing one of the more familiar and ostensibly "natural" types of story, the story that gets its main impetus from its sense of an ending. By writing a novel that satisfies even the most impatient reader's demand for spare, suspenseful plot construction, Pynchon has exposed some of the assumptions implicit in the demand for spareness and suspense. *The Crying of Lot 49* explores and exploits the genre of quest or mystery story so thoroughly that it is in many ways an exemplary narrative. It tests the limits of an extremely traditional pattern, providing a retrospective context for the experiments of *V.* and motivating the explosion of linear form that is both structural principle and theme in *Gravity's Rainbow*.

The Impossibility of (Dis)Closure

Lot 49 is a novel that moves toward its conclusion with maximum efficiency. This conclusion promises to reveal the significance of all the preceding action, and until the conclusion all judgments of significance apparently must be held in abeyance. The culminating revelation can take one of two familiar forms. Either (1) everything adds up to such an absolute unity that it is in the strictest sense unimaginable (Oedipa anticipates a "direct, epileptic Word," p. 87), or (2) there are no connections between events beyond those that Oedipa has wished into existence. As Geoffrey Hartman notes, Pynchon outwits closure in this novel;[3] indeed, given the alternatives, it is difficult to see how Pynchon could have realized either possible conclusion. *Lot 49* is so thoroughly apocalyptic in structure that the final revelation cannot occur. The conclusion is necessarily deferred.

Pynchon has his omniscient narrator spell out the alternative interpretations near the end of the novel, when Oedipa has resigned herself to waiting for the onset of revelation. This passage in effect claims to restrict the permissable readings of *Lot 49* to two. More insidiously, as I shall argue, it guarantees that neither of these readings will receive authorial sanction.

> Behind the hieroglyphic streets there would either be a transcendent meaning, or only the earth. In the songs Miles, Dean, Serge and Leonard sang was either some fraction of the truth's numinous beauty (as Mucho now believed) or only a power spectrum. Tremaine the Swastika Salesman's reprieve from holocaust was either an injustice, or the absence of a wind; the bones of the GI's at the bottom of Lake Inverarity were there either for a reason that mattered to the world, or for skindivers and cigarette smokers. Ones and zeroes. So did the couples arrange themselves. At Vesperhaven House either an accommodation reached, in some kind of dignity, with the Angel of Death, or only death and the daily, tedious preparations for it. Another mode of meaning behind the obvious, or none. Either Oedipa in the orbiting ecstasy of a true paranoia, or a real Tristero. For there either was some Tristero beyond the appearance of the legacy America, or there was just America and if there was just America then it seemed the only way she could continue, and manage to be at all relevant to it, was as an alien, unfurrowed, assumed full circle into some paranoia. (Pp. 136–37)

This evocation of a reality bifurcated into "Ones and zeroes" by alternative interpretations attests to Pynchon's considerable mastery of nuance. Certainly there is a strong *sense* of the options here. It means something to say that experience encodes equally the promise of "transcendent meaning, or only the earth"; the choice is clearly between All and Nothing, a universe pregnant with purposes for the meanest and most apparently gratuitous life or, on the contrary, a universe in which there is no meaning anywhere, for anyone. The polarized alternatives set up an enormous amount of tension within the book.

But it is also difficult to specify how these options could be realized. What does the world look like, for instance, when it is infused with "transcendent meaning"? How does one grasp "another mode of meaning behind the obvious"? What mode? What is the obvious? Pynchon's expansions on this theme are always cryptic. A miracle, the Mexican anarchist Jesus Arrabal tells Oedipa, is "another world's intrusion into this one" (p. 88). But what is this other world? Pynchon presses at the borders of what the novelist Carlos Casteneda has called "a separate reality" without indulging Casteneda's unfortunate penchant for mapping this "reality" in excessively literalistic terms, on top of largely familiar terrain. As a result, his insinuations remain haunting. They remain vague.

The other pole of the dichotomy is equally difficult to imagine. If there is no transcendent meaning, then there is "only the earth." But what is that? Or, for that matter, "only a power spectrum," or "just America"? The implication is: less than you think. But again, *how* does a world appear when it is "just" what it is? Can it appear at all if it is devoid of meaning? Can it appear devoid of meaning in a novel?[4] These are not quibbling questions because the polarized alternatives are brought forth as the only conclusions the novel can have. Oedipa *will* know a transfigured world, rendered wholly other than the world she now perceives; either that, or she *will* find herself in a world stripped of all values and meanings and reduced to absolute fragmentation. Within the covers of *The Crying of Lot 49*, however, she never achieves the culminating insight into the nature of her world, and thus neither interpretation receives authorial sanction.

Each of the possible "resolutions" promises to change the aspect of the preceding action so completely that the whole story seems on the brink of becoming unintelligible. A world redeemed by "pulsing stelliferous Meaning" (p. 58) promises to be totally different from the world in which Oedipa encounters the septuagenarian Mr. Thoth, the peculiar organization known as Inamorati Anonymous, and the old, alcoholic sailor. Each of these encounters is poignant because it accentuates a sense of waste and loss and emphasizes the deficiencies of a society that persistently overlooks certain of its members. But if this society is comprehended by a larger and ultimately redemptive system—if apparent loss is an index of actual salvation—these incidents lose their pathos. Contemplating the sailor, Oedipa is startled into a recognition of mortality: "It was as if she had just discovered the irreversible process" (p. 95). But the structure of the novel insinuates that this recognition is only a step along her way; it exists only to be transformed in light of a final revelation. If this revelation integrates Oedipa's experience in a full understanding of how everything fits, such a "transcendent meaning" will negate the pathos of her discovery. Her whole quest will emerge as a process of misapprehension, culminating in a reversal in which apparent waste is transmuted into real gold. Alternatively, if this revelation confirms the essential meaninglessness of her world, her discovery too will be meaningless. Either way, the entirety of the action is so completely oriented toward an apocalyptic "end" (in the dual sense of "terminus" and "fulfillment") that it seems Oedipa's world exists for the purpose of being changed utterly. Pynchon carefully refrains from trying to specify what it might change into.

In other words, Pynchon has projected twin "resolutions" to this second novel that cannot be realized within the novel. He has done this with deliberation and artistry, so that the narrative appears thoroughly teleological, moving nowhere but forward, motivated entirely by its sense of an ending. For this reason *The Crying of Lot 49* is an elegant, concise, and economical narrative, a paradigm of unencumbered linear development. Yet it does not come to the conclusion it anticipates. And this fact seems almost a betrayal because Pynchon continually stresses that the conclusion is what the whole narrative is for. His ruling convention in this novel seems to be that the action remains in a state of pure potency until it receives a baptism of cosmic significance—or of cosmic insignificance, as the case may be—at the close. This convention dictates that in the absence of a definitive resolution the whole story ought to freeze into an attitude of waiting, with the possibility of meaning permanently deferred. It should be impossible to discuss what "happens" in the novel except in a highly provisional way, for in *Lot 49*'s own terms, what "happens" is wholly contingent on whether Oedipa's world is charged with "transcendent meaning" or whether, on the contrary, it is "only the earth." *Lot 49* should be a fragment, not a novel at all. But at this point conventional habits of reading break down: to take seriously the ostensible deferral of the conclusion is to deny *Lot 49*'s integrity. *Lot 49* does mean; furthermore, it is an aesthetic unity. It is both meaningful and whole *because* it does not affirm an ultimate interpretation of its own reality.

An ultimate interpretation would be beside the point. Anyone fumbling for a climactic statement of what *Lot 49* adds up to might consider Alexander Pope's optimistic solution to the problem of waste and suffering, "All partial Evil, universal Good,"[5] or the observation to which John Barth nearly commits his hero at the end of *The Floating Opera*, "If nothing makes any final difference, that fact makes no final difference either."[6] The blanket affirmation of either a benignly purposive order or of an indifferently meaningless chaos tends to be thuddingly anticlimactic.[7] Besides being vague and vacuous, such affirmations only cheapen the preceding action by making this action merely an accessory to the conclusion, a means to an end.

Yet *Lot 49* undeniably gets its impetus from the lure of a closure that is also a disclosure. It moves forward drawn by the powerful desire it has created for an explanation that will cover everything that has occurred. It is no less a quest narrative because its goal, or grail, never puts in an appearance. On the contrary, it both epitomizes and parodies the genre of quest narrative by virtue of the fact that it withholds its object from view. In the process it calls attention to the paradoxical nature of goals and grails in quest literature, for by convention the quest object never fulfills the quest, never satisfies the desire its absence arouses.

Quest and Wasteland

With remarkable narrative economy, the opening sentence of *The Crying of Lot 49* immediately establishes the direction of the ensuing action:

> One summer afternoon Mrs Oedipa Maas came home from a Tupperware party whose hostess had put perhaps too much kirsch in the fondue to find that she, Oedipa, had been named executor, or she supposed executrix, of the estate of one Pierce Inverarity, a California real estate mogul who had once lost two million dollars in his spare time but still had assets numerous and tangled enough to make the job of sorting it all out more than honorary.

This sentence evokes both Oedipa's context ("a Tupperware party whose hostess had put perhaps too much kirsch in the fondue") and the context of her appointed task ("the estate of one Pierce Inverarity, a California real estate mogul who had once lost two million dollars in his spare time"). It thus grounds the quest in a hyperbolically banalized world. At the same time, it propels Oedipa upward, out of this banality: like Venus emerging from the sea, she is already rising from a "Californicated" level of existence into a new life. Her quest is a birth-passage, and from the beginning she is directed toward transcendence. Her subsequent progress is cumulative and linear. She is never deflected from her course; nothing that happens to her is irrelevant to her thesis that an omnipotent Tristero-system presides over seemingly random attempts at communication. Only one blocking action impedes her quest, and this is the suspicion that the promise of transcendence may be a complete illusion. The Tristero may not exist. Pynchon thus resolves the quest formula into its essential components: one hero, one goal, one obstacle.

He also allows the suggestion of transcendence to take on the full range of metaphysical and religious connotations associated with the quest pattern. Oedipa hopes to emerge from the darkness of her received ideas into the light of truth; she longs for "the cry that might abolish the night" (p. 87). Her name, which is initially merely ludicrous, loses its associations with Freudian trendiness as the quest proceeds, and begins to recall her truth-seeking Sophoclean predecessor. The letter that precipitates her journey portends a conclusion, sending Oedipa in pursuit of an absolute whose nature she is radically unsure of. It also signals a pattern of potentially revelatory messages, reminding her of the mysterious long-distance call that Inverarity had made a year previously and looking forward to the auctioneer's "crying" that promises or threatens to dispel all mystery. In this eschatologically charged atmosphere, there is a strong suggestion that the final "crying" is analogous to another culminating summons, the sounding of the Last Trump: blown, perhaps, on the Tristero's symbolic post horn, unmuted at last.

The structure of the narrative is thus overtly apocalyptic. It moves toward a conclusion that is also a revelation and augurs a complete transformation of the novel's world. If this world is initially vapid and banal, Oedipa's progress serves in part to restore it, for Oedipa rises above her vacuous reality by interpreting aspects of that reality as signs. Her first view of the city of San Narciso, "a vast sprawl of houses which had grown up all together, like a well-tended crop, from the dull brown earth," suggests a "hieroglyphic sense of concealed meaning, of an intent to communicate" (p. 13). An apparent misprint in a cancellation message alerts her to the possibility of subversive elements undermining the U.S. Post Office (p. 30). A message on a latrine wall is her first clue to the alternative W.A.S.T.E. postal system, and the same graffito introduces her to the symbol of the muted post horn (p. 34). Acquaintance with a member of a Southern California "right-wing nut outfit" provides her with information about the federal government's efforts to suppress independent mail services (pp. 35–36), and a subsequent visit to one of Inverarity's housing developments suggests a possible connection between salvaged human skeletons and the Jacobean revenge tragedy being produced by a Little Theater group (pp. 43–44). The play yields a name, "Trystero," that seems to provide a center to the interwoven references. Apparently trivial, random discoveries display phantom resemblances that make them potentially important and purposive; these resemblances will be meaningful, Oedipa believes, if they point to a shadowy force or presence behind them. By the end of the third chapter, events have to a large extent justified the passage of foreshadowing that begins the chapter: "That's what would come to haunt her most, perhaps; the way it fitted, logically, together. As if (as she'd guessed that first minute in San Narciso) there were revelation in progress all around her" (p. 28).

By insinuating that Oedipa's parodically conceived world is made up of signs, Pynchon effectively begins a process of debanalizing this world. His strategy is to manipulate an established satiric device so that it serves purposes other than satire. The hyperbolically rendered details of everyday California life—the tract housing concept brought to fruition as a whole city of houses "grown up together," the bathroom graffiti impersonally soliciting sexual partners, the human bones transformed to serve smokers and skindivers, the Little Theater's attempts to introduce Jacobean revenge and betrayal into a sterile Orange County landscape—are conventionally synecdochic. Initially, at least, their function is to point out the absurdity and incoherence of mid-century America. They are "slices" of a life that makes little sense, and as "slices" they are purely descriptive, designed to evoke an atmosphere.

Such patches of exaggerated local color are the satirist's version of the "descriptive residue" that Jonathan Culler, following Roland Barthes, discusses in *Structuralist Poetics*: "items whose only apparent role in the text is that of denoting a concrete reality (trivial gestures, insignificant objects, superfluous dialogue)."[8] They are indications of a brute level of reality that eludes characters' efforts to discover meaning, or even hints of what existentialists have termed an "opaque" realm of being that is irreconcilable to the human desire for significance. By rendering such details parodically, the satirist exploits the function they serve in traditional realistic fiction. They signal a resistance to meaning. When this resistance is heightened by parody, it becomes the absurd.

But Pynchon plants his conventionally absurd "bits" only to question their apparent absurdity. He uses the device of the "descriptive residue" to initiate a radical questioning of whether anything can be merely residue. One of his overriding themes in *Lot 49* is that officially defined waste is potentially fertile. The underground postal system that Oedipa discovers is called W.A.S.T.E., and the name allows the syndicate's mailboxes to pass as garbage cans. Only the barely perceptible periods between letters indicate that the word is an acronym, for We Await Silent Tristero's Empire. The W.A.S.T.E. baskets become emblematic of Oedipa's progress, for in the course of her quest, she discovers a "wasted" population linked by an elaborate system of communication and by a common attitude of waiting, as if for a coming millenium. She grows more attentive to the significance of elements that her dominant culture has written off: the barely perceptible incongruities begin to leap out at her and to suggest new levels of correspondence. And as she moves toward an impending resolution, the tone of the narration becomes less evidently parodic. Episodes like her interview with Mr. Thoth, the elderly convalescent who cannot distinguish his childhood memories from Porky Pig cartoons, are both evocative and pathetic, but not occasions for laughter: waste clearly signifies by this point in the story, and Mr. Thoth's confusion, like his name, represents another code to be cracked, revealing another part or aspect of the central message.

Waste signifies; it communicates. "Communication is the key," cries the inventor John Nefastis (p. 77); and Oedipa dutifully takes this slogan as her cue to intuit an order behind apparent chaos, or perhaps to impose such an order on a meaningless reality. "*Shall I project a world?*" she asks herself near the novel's midpoint (p. 59), and the question has ominous implications. In Freudian terms to project is to attribute personal hopes and fears to an external object; in existentialist terms it is to interpret present reality in light of a future goal.[9] As Oedipa comes to suspect, such projection is equivalent to paranoia and at her stage amounts to cosmic error. If she has projected meaning and value onto her world merely because she wants her world to have meaning and value, she is hallucinating, and worse, the world is wholly alien: "only the earth." It communicates nothing. As she sees it, if her "project," the Tristero, does not exist, the codes break down. The signs point to nothing at all.

But this conclusion presumes that if waste communicates, its sole message must be that the Tristero lurks in the background manipulating signs, like the Augustinian God whose elaborate Creation functions as a text attesting to his agency. Either the "residue" of Oedipa's experience means that the Tristero exists, or it does not mean. Oedipa operates on this assumption throughout the book, and because she is the central character, and a very sympathetic character, she offers a persuasive paradigm of interpretation. But her example is finally parodic. As the plot develops, the question of the Tristero's existence or nonexistence becomes beside the point.

The overt purpose of the parody in *Lot 49* is to show that Oedipa's world is deficient. This deficiency is not a static quality: in the course of the narration it becomes more and more evidently a lack, a state of neediness, so that parody is not an end in itself but a ritualized "crying" for absolute fulfillment. But as Pynchon allows the initial level of parody to be muted into pathos, he emphasizes another less obvious level of parody. Oedipa's world cries out for so much meaning that the novel cannot reasonably be expected to satisfy it. Pynchon possesses no Grail that will fulfill his hero's, or his readers', expectations. But this problem is intrinsic to the structure of the quest narrative. A characteristic feature of such narratives is that they cannot make good their own promises in any literalistic fashion. Climactic revelation tends to be beyond the reach of description or explanation.[10] In his handling of this condition, Pynchon is able to satirize the assumption that a narrative means only when it adds up to a culminating insight. In the process he explores the complex and incomplete ways in which even an apparently straightforward, teleological, linear narrative does mean.

The framing narrator of Conrad's great quest narrative *Heart of Darkness* observes of the storyteller Marlow, "to him the meaning of an eposide was not inside like a kernel but outside, enveloping the tale which brought it out only as a glow brings out a haze, in the likeness of one of those misty halos that sometimes are made visible by the spectral illumination of moonshine."[11] Pynchon offers no such hints, and no nesting boxes of narrators suggest that in *Lot 49* things are not quite what they appear and that meaning may not be hiding in the obvious places. But in orienting all his action toward the missing kernel of significance, he operates like a sleight-of-hand man, misdirecting attention and arousing a desire for a core, center, culmination, end that has never existed. Paradoxically, *Lot 49* appears elegant, economical, and thoroughly traditional insofar as it promises to do something that no novel has ever done: it promises to utter the "direct, epileptic Word," the definitive revelation of what everything signifies. When it fails to utter this Word—when the auctioneer's "crying" inaugurates only silence—the novel assumes its final shape, and, as in *Heart of Darkness*, the supposedly withheld meaning becomes an enveloping haze, which the glow of the story illumines.

As the narrative proceeds, the hypothesized Tristero assumes more definition, until it is relatively clear what kind of thing it is that Oedipa expects to find. But this clarity is subversive. As the Tristero acquires shape—as it gains a genesis, a membership, and a motive—it loses its potential for comprehensiveness. As it becomes identifiable, it becomes explicable. And this development appears inevitable, for in novelistic terms to reveal is to define, or set limits. Like the traditional questing hero, Oedipa loses her companions as she approaches her elusive Grail, but her progressive alienation parallels a progressive diminution of the Grail itself. If the Tristero is to appear in the novel, it must somehow be commensurate to the novel's world. Anything that can be seen must be seeable in terms of the ruling aesthetic conventions: Wagner's Parsifal uncovers a large, backlit cup.

In the same way, the Tristero becomes historicized and thus diminished as it is assimilated to the historical continuum of *Lot 49*'s world. The effect of the word *Trystero*, articulated only once in *The Courier's Tragedy*, intrigues Oedipa, but it provokes her to disentangle the Tristero from its stage trappings. In the process she demystifies it. Her research turns up a great deal of information: the Tristero originated with a rebellion against the Thurn and Taxis family's postal monopoly; it emigrated to America and was responsible for certain "Indian" attacks against the Pony Express; it persists as the W.A.S.T.E.system, an underground and illegal alternative to the U.S. mail. But these clues tend to assimilate the Tristero to the world of the novel, so that if it exists, it will not be "another world's intrusion into this one" but an aspect of this world—an overlooked aspect, but one that is not completely different. If the Tristero turns out to exist, it will be a secret society with a long history of petty swipes against established systems of communication.

Such a secret society does not seem to be the sort of thing

that can infuse "transcendent meaning" into a sterile and banal world. But by the time the Tristero has assumed historical definition, its redemptive power is no longer at issue. Oedipa's world has acquired its own meaning and value in the course of the quest. And with its progressive diminution, the Tristero has become correspondingly more human: fragile, contingent, and, paradoxically, in need of Oedipa's care and protection. It acquires these characteristics because it becomes identified with a level of human reality that Oedipa has previously overlooked. It becomes a sign itself, pointing toward a community of solitaries who in establishment terms do not signify because they do not fit into an officially acknowledged system. Oedipa begins to think in terms of a "Tristero system" that links alienated and dispossessed people by giving them a *telos* in a kind of ideal community, a City of God. But in seeing this outcast population as a means to an end, she overlooks the links that already bind them together: their shared alienation and dispossession. Waste communicates, but Oedipa overlooks its message. If the signs do not herald the coming of Silent Tristero's Empire, she believes she must regard them as meaningless babble.

Missed Messages, Excluded Middles

The Crying of Lot 49 is thus not only the story of Oedipa's quest but the story of what Oedipa misses or discounts because she is on a quest. The novel comprehends what she passes over as well as what she construes as evidence; it includes her exclusions. Inverarity's legacy to Oedipa is finally identified as America (p. 134), but ironically the tradition that Oedipa has already inherited keeps her from taking possession of her own reality. This tradition has emigrated, like the Tristero, from an older European culture; but in America it takes a peculiarly extreme form, espousing the myth of a New Jerusalem on the one hand, and on the other hand denying that any community at all can exist. America was a land of possibility for its founders, but this possibility was defined in terms of an errand into the wilderness, a providential mission. Either America existed to be redeemed by the Second Coming, or it was unredeemable. Lacking faith, Oedipa fears the second alternative; in the absence of an eschaton, she retreats into Romantic solipsism. If the world will not be informed by a "pulsing stelliferous Meaning" that is qualitatively different from mere lower-case "meaning," her impulse is to assume that all meaning is an illusion. By her own metaphor, she is a princess in a tower, projecting the cohesive system of interpretations that she calls the world over a void.

This metaphor for Oedipa's situation occurs at the end of chapter one, and effectively sets up the subsequent action. Thinking back on her affair with Inverarity, Oedipa recalls a painting of beautiful girls,

> prisoners in the top room of a circular tower, embroidering a kind of tapestry which spilled out the slit windows and into a void, seeking hopelessly to fill the void: for all the other buildings and creatures, all the waves, ships and forests of the earth were contained in this tapestry, and the tapestry was the world. (P. 10)[12]

The painting sums up the case for Romantic despair. "Lift not the painted veil which those who live / Call Life," Shelley implored; and Oedipa, confronted by a vision of her own world as the product of her own solipsistic "embroidering," realizes that in this case there can be no escape: "If the tower is everywhere and the knight of deliverance no proof against its magic, what else?" (pp. 10–11).

But "what else?" is not a rhetorical question, for there is something else: the world of shared meanings that she is to discover, distinct from both the tapestry of significance that can be real only if a real Tristero does the embroidery and the "void" that lurks behind it. This world lacks the coherence of a myth that moves toward a projected fulfillment, but it is not incoherent. It means something that this world lacks unity, purpose, and redemptive significance; ironically, it is this meaning that Oedipa discovers during her quest, although she never realizes that this meaning keeps her legacy from being threatened by total meaninglessness. "And how had it ever happened here, with the chances once so good for diversity?" is a question for America, which has effectively denied possibility by bifurcating its population into members of an authorized "order" or waste. But it is also a question for Oedipa, who has duplicated America's error by judging that if the Tristero does not somehow provide a transcendent purpose for suffering and alienation, then humanity in its entirety is detritus. She has assimilated her legacy without recognizing it. Like America, she fails to see the alternatives.

Pynchon, however, dramatizes the alternatives by having the parodic, banal world that Oedipa inhabits gradually take on depth and seriousness in light of the transcendent that she seeks. Oedipa's California, initially a composite of clichés and "characteristic" gestures—a figured surface—grows more intrinsically interesting as Oedipa tries to "read" it for evidence of the Tristero's omnipresence. Thoroughly unknown initially, the Tristero can function as both threat and promise: it may come as redeemer or as exterminating angel; but in either case it signals radical, unimaginable transformation. It figures first as a level of innuendo, suggesting apocalyptic resonances in the cliché- and jargon-ridden speech of the characters:

> "You think like a Bircher," Fallopian said. "Good guys and bad guys. You never get to any of the underlying truth. Sure he was against industrial capitalism. So are we. Didn't it lead, inevitably, to Marxism? Underneath, both are part of the same creeping horror."
> "Industrial *anything*," hazarded Metzger.
> "There you go," nodded Fallopian. (P. 33)

The Tristero is always associated with extremes: with Fallopian's extreme right-wing political stance, for instance, which modulates into an extreme left-wing political stance without ever becoming completely intelligible within the novel's world. Oedipa's yearning for "pulsing stelliferous Meaning" (p. 58) is another rendering of the extreme; Arrabal's hypothesized "miracle" is yet another. By manipulating such evocative moments, Pynchon is able to make the Tristero the form of a final, apocalyptic message without ever suggesting what the content of this message might be. "Is this the promis'd end?" Kent cries in the last scene of *King Lear*, but Edgar adds the sensible qualification, "Or image of that horror?" It is the image, of course, that makes the horror palpable. Pynchon's sleight-of-hand in *Lot 49* involves promising the end without ever providing an image of it. The Tristero is always associated with the idea of communication; as a postal service, it is a vehicle for messages, and in her quest Oedipa assumes that it will constitute the culminating, definitive message by itself. But though "Communication is the key" to the Tristero, *what* is communicated is disproportionate to the Tristero's sense of promise. After an enormous buildup introducing the W.A.S.T.E. system, Oedipa is allowed to read a letter that has come through officially unauthorized channels:

> *Dear Mike*, it said, *how are you? Just thought I'd drop you a note. How's your book coming? Guess that's all for now. See you at The Scope.* (P. 35)

The Tristero itself threatens to be such an anticlimax.

Parodic and anagogic elements war in the early part of the book, and the outcome is usually comic deflation. Like the insistently punning names of the characters—Manny diPresso, Mike Fallopian, Stanley Koteks, Genghis Cohen, Dr. Hilarius, Randolph Driblette—this sort of humor wears thin quickly, and Pynchon appears to risk charges of triviality by raising his readers' expectations only to dash them time and time again. But *Lot 49* is not a trivial novel, and the reason is that all this comic deflation sets the scene for the ensuing action. Neither parody nor anagogy contains much potential for development: the first three chapters articulate a need for a level of reality that falls somewhere in between. In the subsequent narration, the two poles begin to converge. The Tristero becomes more finite and more nearly human; Oedipa's sterile world becomes more intelligible and worthy of compassion. The tone of narration stops swinging between the extremes of cosmic meaning and total meaninglessness and settles down to vibrating on a middle frequency. *The Crying of Lot 49* becomes a realistic novel as it develops, and its emergent realism subsumes the initial question of whether the Tristero does or does not exist.

The stages of Oedipa's quest raise her world almost imperceptibly; at the same time, they lower the status of the Tristero. When Oedipa talks to the director of *The Courier's Tragedy*, Randolph Driblette, she is preoccupied with the significance of the word Driblette added to the text, "Trystero," and disposed to disregard his disclaimer: "But the reality is in *this* head. Mine. I'm the projector at the planetarium, all the closed little universe visible in the circle of that stage is coming out of my mouth, eyes, sometimes other orifices also" (p. 56). This explanation would seem to make Driblette himself a projector of worlds, as Oedipa herself may be an embroiderer of tapestries, and she cannot bear to have her vision of total alienation confirmed. But Driblette is saying something different and talking past her overt concerns to the motive underlying them, her sense of isolation.

> "Driblette?" Oedipa called, after awhile.
> His face appeared briefly. "We could do that." He wasn't smiling. His eyes waited, at the centres of their webs.
> "I'll call," said Oedipa. (P. 57)

She does not call; later she learns that Driblette has killed himself. In seeking the Word, Oedipa misses the message. The pattern haunts her quest. The Tristero may represent a promise of absolute community—this is what she yearns for, and this is the fulfillment of the key concept, communication. But in ignoring Driblette's invitation, Oedipa overlooks the basis for a real community that could include her: a shared sense of loneliness and longing. She is attracted to Driblette, but has more important matters to attend to. She moves on into increasing isolation.

Her subsequent encounters play out essentially the same scenario, except that she is increasingly moved by the situations of the people she meets and increasingly confused by how many elements of these situations she must discount if she is to look only for clues to the Tristero. Her interviews with Stanley Koteks, Mr. Thoth, Genghis Cohen, and John Nefastis yield a perplexing quantity of information, much of it *about* the problem of separating information from irrelevant "noise."[13] But Oedipa construes such messages only in terms of her fear of solipsism, and allows even the lesson of her experience with the Nefastis Machine to elude her. The Nefastis Machine, according to its inventor, contains a genuine Maxwell's Demon who can sort data so that it yields meaningful information if activated by a "sensitive." Oedipa tries out her sensitivity and fails. The message, as Nefastis had observed, is in the metaphor: in her progress toward presumed revelation, she has failed all along as a sorting demon because she has persistently rejected the elements of her experience that signal meaning and value in her own world. She is struck by compassion and empathy in each of her encounters with these solitary and perversely endearing characters, but she avoids identification, refuses to rest in compassion, and continues her journey toward what she hopes is transcendence.

A late stage of this journey is implicitly its climax. Frightened by the implications of her discoveries about the Tristero, Oedipa decides to give herself up to chance and, by wandering through the streets of San Francisco, to give the Tristero an opportunity to reveal itself. By this time she is wary of her own obsession, and hopes "there might still be a chance of getting the whole thing to go away and disintegrate quietly.

She had only to drift tonight, at random, and watch nothing happen, to be convinced it was purely nervous, a little something for her shrink to fix'' (p. 80). She sets out to "watch nothing happen" and ends up seeing everything. Or, more accurately, she discovers that it is impossible to watch nothing happen: "nothing," the implicit backdrop for her former banal life, is full of import. She sees the world behind the tapestry and finds that it is not a void. But she does not understand what she sees because she is looking only for evidence of the Tristero.

The Tristero does not reveal itself during Oedipa's dark night on the streets of San Francisco. Instead, it reveals other things previously beneath her concern. The post horn symbol flickers through a panorama of images, leading her down a labyrinthine path that intersects with the secret paths of countless other people, recalling her attention from the future, where revelation presumably waits, to the immediate present. In essence, she gets a guided tour of the human condition, and finds it too vast, too diverse, and too familiar to comprehend. As she plays "the voyeur and listener" Oedipa frantically tries to put things together, to project a resolution that will gather up all these aspects of her experience and reconcile intolerable diversity into complete unity. As self-ordained sleuth, she feels obliged to make things add up, and in this way to solve the mystery of human existence once and for all. But the strain of holding things together is too much; she succumbs to information overload.

> But the private eye sooner or later has to get beat up on. This night's profusion of post horns, this malignant, deliberate replication, was their way of beating up. They knew her pressure points, and the ganglia of her optimism, and one by one, pinch by precision pinch, they were immobilizing her. (Pp. 91–92)

In trying to transform her night's adventures into some kind of explanatory system, Oedipa effectively denies that she is part of what she perceives. Because she aims at complete transcendence, she keeps construing events as clues that will carry her forward, away from humanity, toward a supernatural level of being that subsumes humanity to its own inscrutable purposes. "I am meant to remember," she reflects. "Each clue that comes is *supposed* to have its own clarity, its fine chances for permanence." But such remembering strikes her as second-best, a poor substitute for the climactic insight that will enfold and explain her discoveries: "But then she wondered if the gemlike 'clues' were only some kind of compensation. To make up for her having lost the direct, epileptic Word, the cry that might abolish the night" (p. 87). In seeking the Word behind the clues, she loses sight of the motive behind her quest. She wants to break out of her tower by discovering a world that is not her own solipsistic creation but still one that offers some place for her desires and needs. She looks for a world that is *like* her. But she does not see how the world she does discover continually reflects back her own image.

A brief incident from the night before her journey through subterranean San Francisco prefigures this failure. Oedipa goes to sleep in her hotel room, but keeps "waking from a nightmare about something in the mirror, across from her bed. Nothing specific, only a possibility, nothing she could see." The dream reflects her quest; her waking reflects its real object: "When she woke in the morning, she was sitting bolt upright, staring into the mirror at her own exhausted face" (p. 74). Oedipa is searching for herself; that is, she is searching for a way to "place" herself in a reality that has always appeared indifferent and alien. Ironically, she is offered the grounds for community in a sense of shared estrangement. Because of her quest, she has discovered a world that is neither indifferent nor alien, but she ignores this information. The Tristero has forced her to see, but she believes she sees only clues to the Tristero.

Her long dark night, the central event of the novel, represents a radical enlargement of her vision. Significantly, it is the episode in the book that is most conspicuously free of parody. The vivid images that Pynchon offers in this section are metaphors for Oedipa's own situation, but they also link Oedipa to a community of people who are all characterized by their isolation. She stumbles on an organization called Inamorati Anonymous, a group of people who have attempted suicide, failed, and recovered, only to swear off love as being inherently too risky. That the Inamorati are a group is essential to the paradox: "Think of it," says the "anonymous inamorato" who tells her the story. "A whole underworld of suicides who failed. All keeping in touch through that secret delivery system. What do they tell each other?" (p. 85).[14] Oedipa does not find out. She moves on, seeing the post horn everywhere among a derelict nighttown population. Each appearance of the symbol directs her to another aspect of the alienation and dispossession that she has acknowledged in herself, as if the post horn were a badge of membership or mark of Cain. She even meets characters engaged in versions of her own enterprise:

> an aging night-watchman, nibbling at a bar of Ivory Soap, who had trained his virtuoso stomach to accept also lotions, air-fresheners, fabrics, tobaccoes and waxes in a hopeless attempt to assimilate it all, all the promise, productivity, betrayal, ulcers, before it was too late; and even another voyeur, who hung outside one of the city's still-lighted windows, searching for who knew what specific image. (P. 91)

The post horn is a mark of kinship. It calls attention to the "wasted" elements of American society and suggests that they compose an alternative society, communicating by different means and relaying different messages.

But Oedipa wants a definitive message, and this desire pushes the narrative forward toward a conclusion so loaded with portents that the attentive reader may recognize that it is unrealizable. The pathos and even tragedy that redeem Oedipa's world from banality emerge as a by-product of the quest—as the residue or waste generated by her being-toward transcendence. Construed as a series of clues pointing to an omnipresent Tristero, her insights reveal the human condition as a state of neediness or deprivation. Oedipa assumes, however, that this neediness and deprivation can be real only if the Tristero is real. And if the Tristero declares its reality—if it "comes" to those awaiting it, presumably wielding some version of fire and the sword—it will eradicate human pathos and tragedy by enfolding such transient phenomena within its Word. The culminating Meaning that Oedipa anticipates is supernatural and superhuman. The alternative is total incoherence. Her own expectations exclude a "middle" that would be a human world, based on the shared hopes and fears that are the tenuous connections of community, and rendered contingent and precious by the awesome fact of mortality.

This "middle" realm is the traditional subject matter of the novel. It is the subject matter of *The Crying of Lot 49*, despite the fact that the narrative appears to exist for the purpose of negating the human world entirely. Pynchon himself has "projected" a world, pitting the multiple resonances that his language sets up against an overriding sense of an ending that promises to resolve diversity into a unitary Word, which articulates the absolute and final truth. The Word is withheld. By this apparent fiat, Pynchon plays at guaranteeing the integrity of his narrative. The absence of the Word allows Oedipa's world to exist.

In making his second novel so purely a quest narrative that it threatens to annihilate itself, Pynchon emphasizes that fictional worlds exist because the Word is lacking. They seem necessarily to exist in anticipation of this culminating and revelatory Word, and to be defined in terms of its absence, as if words multiplied in the attempt to achieve some unimaginable wholeness. All novels are "projects" in Sartre's sense; all point forward to an ideal resolution that will reconcile every one of the variegated strands of narrative. But such an ideal resolution has no place *within* the novel. It does not fit because the novel as a genre is also committed to reflecting some aspect of a public reality, and thus committed to incorporating contingency into its structure. Novels do not realize the "promis'd end," although they may provide an image of it.

The ostensible meaning of *Lot 49*'s world does not emerge at the conclusion. Indeed, the conclusion contrives to suggest that no meaning is yet present, and that the tension between Meaning and no-meaning will be prolonged indefinitely:

> An assistant closed the heavy door on the lobby windows and the sun. She heard a lock snap shut; the sound echoed a moment. Passerine spread his arms in a gesture that seemed to belong to the priesthood of some remote culture; perhaps to a descending angel. The auctioneer cleared his throat. Oedipa settled back, to await the crying of lot 49.

With the shutting of the lock, Oedipa returns to her tower, where she is left to contemplate the options of tapestry and void. But these are not the only options that the novel itself offers.

Like all questing heroes, Oedipa has traveled through a wasteland, but her commitment to the quest has prevented her from grasping the fact central to the novel, that waste is precisely what is most valuable. Established systems of organization convert human beings into articles of production or consumption: Oedipa herself appears first as a buyer of Tupperware, tearer of romaine and garlicker of lasagna, reader of *Scientific American*. To be excluded from this cycle, as Oedipa is when she becomes obsessed by her quest, is to be human, and every character in the book perceives himself as somehow excluded. The first thing that Oedipa discovers about each of these characters is that he does not count in some official reckoning. Oedipa herself has to be propelled out of her matronly rounds in order to see these people at all.

The quest provides her with the chance to break out of her tower and to perceive a world officially declared invisible, or "void." But the quest also prompts her to make exclusion from established systems the grounds for inclusion in an incomprehensibly vast Tristero system. With American optimism she sees suffering and alienation and asks, "What good is it?" It must be good *for* something—for the coming of Silent Tristero's Empire, perhaps—or it can have no meaning. The structure of the quest (which is also the overt structure of the novel) forces the dilemma.

But Pynchon's detailed depictions of suffering and alienation in contemporary America are important in themselves, not just insofar as they further the plot. They are what is important, in fact. As the quest develops, Oedipa's world begins to provoke more compassion. Meaning seeps out from the interstices of the text: the interest of Mr. Thoth, the old sailor, and even the ill-fated Driblette does not lie in the clues each provides but in the meticulous thumbnail sketch of an individual life that Pynchon offers in each case. These are developed characters, and Oedipa's willingness to use them and then dispose of them suggests that she is still synced into the American dream. She does not value waste. She moves relentlessly toward the conclusion.

But as the narrative moves forward, it leaves a mass of "descriptive residue" in its wake, and this residue constitutes a world. Oedipa apprehends her reality as poised on the brink of becoming either All or Nothing. As she proceeds, however, this reality gains shape and solidity. It eludes banality by becoming distinctive and concrete, and its growing definition makes it increasingly impervious to symbolic intimations of a coming apocalypse. Furthermore, it communicates. It elicits sympathy and even identification from both Oedipa and the reader. And it communicates Pynchon's bleakly compassionate vision of present-day America as a community of isolates, all of them in communication with others, and communicating the fact of their solitude.

The idea of a community of isolates is a paradox. Oedipa cannot deal with it: either the isolation is so complete that people can take no notice of one another, or a superior force

coordinates individual realities so that solipsists move un-
knowingly and unwillingly toward a common goal in accordance with a preestablished harmony. Pulled into a dance of
deaf-mutes, where "each couple on the floor danced whatever
was in the fellow's head: tango, two-step, bossa nova, slop,"
she reflects, "There would have to be collisions. The only
alternative was some unthinkable order of music, many
rhythms, all keys at once, a choreography in which each
couple meshed easy, predestined" (p. 97). But the fact that
there are no collisions is no evidence for predestination. Unlike Leibnizian monads,[15] the deaf-mutes interact; they must
communicate as a condition for their coexistence. In the same
way, the isolates that Oedipa discovers communicate, although their means of communication generally escapes
notice. The fact of communication, not some coming Tristero
system, links the disparate elements of Oedipa's world and
guarantees that no one is really alone in a tower. It allows
isolates to insist on their isolation. It allows the princess in the
tower to be an object on display at a national museum—a
public fantasy.

This vision of contemporary reality is not the official meaning of *The Crying of Lot 49*. The official meaning is deferred.
What is left is only a by-product of the quest: a world.
Pynchon has exploited the narrative's inherent resistance to
closure, its tendency to generate implications that cannot be
reconciled to a definitive interpretation, to suggest that the
novelist projects a world by his refusal to articulate a single
comprehensive Word. World is antithetical to Word, but made
up of words. Such a world does not yield Meaning, but is a
complex of overlapping meanings. By projecting a world, the
novelist provides a context in which events do not have to be
explained by reference to an ultimate purpose or, in the
absence of such a purpose, declared inexplicable. But
Pynchon has also exploited the teleology inherent in the form
of the quest narrative to insist that in the absence of a conclusion, the book has come to nothing. Because it falls short of

"pulsing stelliferous Meaning," it is waste. The fact that waste communicates is the joke, and the reason why *Lot 49*'s structural purity emerges as parody.

4

The Arc and the Convenant:
Gravity's Rainbow as Secular History

> About the paranoia often noted under the drug, there is nothing
> remarkable. Like other sorts of paranoia, it is nothing less than
> the onset, the leading edge, of the discovery that *everything is
> connected*, everything in the Creation, a secondary illumina-
> tion—not yet blindingly One, but at least connected, and perhaps
> a route In for those like Tchitcherine who are held at the edge....
> (P. 703, Pynchon's ellipsis)

Gravity's Rainbow itself seems held at the edge of discovery. In its encyclopedic scope, the novel appears dedicated to the proposition that *everything is connected*: there are
insinuated links between synthetic polymerization and the
evolution of the earth; between astrophysics and psychic
phenomena; between African dialects and Rilkean poetics;
between international cartels and Freemasonry; between
comic books and covenant theology; between Orphism,
Parsifalism, Tannhaüserism, and *The Autobiography of
Malcolm X*; between German idealism, Pavlovian psychology,
and the American cult of the good-guy loner. Just as these
links could be extended, so the connections reach out in all
directions, associating disparate bodies of knowledge in such
intricate configurations that the universe seems on the point of
cohering like a giant molecule dreamed by some macrocosmic
Kekulé. But the novel remains at the level of secondary illumination and leading edges. The synthetic dream never
occurs. The text refuses to yield a culminating vision of the
universe as "blindingly One."

The totalizing tendency of the thematic connections is so pronounced that this refusal might appear simply perverse. Scott Simmon has speculated that *Gravity's Rainbow* is a novel in which things are more important than people and ideas are more important than things,[1] and his observation suggests that Pynchon's third novel is more committed to a purely conceptual model of coherence than either of the previous works. Both *V.* and *Lot 49* offer something that looks like a conventional narrative as a guiding thread through their labyrinths of thematic complication, although both books ultimately subvert the integrity of the narrative. *Gravity's Rainbow*, on the other hand, introduces a panorama of characters and an unstable narrative voice in its opening pages, thwarting expectations of conventional narrative continuity. The unity of this novel accordingly should derive from its controlling vision—from what one critic has termed the Big Idea.[2] But although it cannot be denied that *Gravity's Rainbow* is a novel of ideas, it is far less clear what these ideas add up to.

The problem is not simply that the novel is fiendishly complex, or that it frequently takes a parodic attitude toward the multiple theories it purveys. Both of these characteristics are common to the encyclopedic narrative, a genre that Ronald T. Swigger has defined in terms of "the drive toward comprehensive knowledge and schematization."[3] This drive to contain and schematize is one of the salient features of *Gravity's Rainbow*; most of the book's rhetoric agitates for a central insight, a route In. But at the same time, an opposed, centrifugal tendency seems to be sending information flying outward like the alternative Zones of the novel's postwar reconstruction, speeding "away from all the others, in fated acceleration, red-shifting, fleeing the Center" (p. 519). This decentralizing tendency is especially apparent in the closing chapter, where even the discrete sections of an already convoluted action begin to fragment into shorter and less obviously related segments with titles like "LISTENING TO THE TOILET, "

"WITTY REPARTEE," "HEART-TO-HEART, MAN-TO-MAN," and "SOME CHARACTERISTICS OF IMI-POLEX G." This marked diffusion of the narrative energy so near the conclusion suggests that the text is thematically committed to incompleteness. The fact that ostensibly central concerns fail to achieve any sort of resolution reinforces this suggestion. Fundamental enigmas—the nature of Slothrop's relation to the Mystery Stimulus, the direction and target of Blicero's Last Firing, the purpose of the Hereros' rocket—are either left ambiguous or dropped entirely. Problematic knots in the plot refuse to unravel, and thus no dénouement—literally, an "untying"—can occur. As the narrator declares on the first page, "this is not a disentanglement from, but a progressive *knotting into*—" (p. 3).

Yet *Gravity's Rainbow* dictates the terms on which totalization should be possible, even as it resists totalization. It appears to place itself within modernist tradition by offering itself as a metaphoric novel, which derives its ultimate coherence from a governing structural metaphor (the commonplace comparison is with *Ulysses*). The "gravity's rainbow" of the title is the arc of the V-2 rocket, which with its sharply defined origin and terminus could claim to be the twentieth century's model of linearity: according to the general theory of relativity, the Euclidean straight line is warped into a curve by the presence of a gravitational field. In many ways this curve shapes the novel. The opening sentence, "A screaming comes across the sky," describes the birth-cry of the supersonic missile heralding the first V-2 offensive on London during September of 1944. On the closing page the final rocket is poised above the heads of "us," and the switch to direct address implies that this rocket's menace is universal. These two events become the extremes of a historical trajectory, containing the labyrinthine plot while acting as exaggerated external pointers to a "rising action" and a "falling action." The structural metaphor is therefore linear, teleological, and deterministic. The parabolic path of the rocket is "that shape of no surprise, no second chances, no return'' (p. 209).[4] To the extent that it controls and structures the novel, this parabola encodes a unified vision of a world hurtling toward annihilation and signifies what Josephine Hendin has called the message of the book, "the death at the heart of all experience."[5]

The parabola is also a metaphor *for* control and structure. It represents the kind of conceptual system that human beings use to circumscribe and rationalize their experience in order to take charge of it. The irony that Pynchon explores in *Gravity's Rainbow* is that such a system always betrays its creators by claiming autonomy for itself. The more comprehensive the structure, the more likely it is to look like fate, so that humanity finds itself serving an antihuman Higher Purpose when it is seduced by the clarity and coherence of its own explanations. The implicit model for all such totalizing systems is the myth of the providential plan, which purports to account for all aspects of human life by directing history to a predetermined end.[6] With the development of science and technology, this myth has become increasingly ironized: historical processes remain inevitable, but the goal of the system is its own destruction. By unifying experience within a controlling vision, humanity has arrived at a model of universal coherence that makes freedom impossible and annihilation imminent.

Although this revised version of the providential myth is overtly nihilistic, it is intellectually persuasive because it appears to explain everything. The lure of totality is so great, Pynchon suggests, that people will assent to a system in which *"everything is connected"* even if the system guarantees their destruction. The culminating irony is that to assent to such a system is to internalize its assumptions and thus to help translate it into reality. In accepting the parabola as the shape of destiny, humanity has simply modified a familiar constellation of beliefs, so that it addresses the inscrutable gods of technology with the old quietistic maxim, "Thy will be done."

But although *Gravity's Rainbow* takes a pessimistic view of the twentieth century's flight into totalizing systems, it also insists that such systems do not have intrinsic authority; they are not imposed on humanity from "outside." No matter how comprehensive the explanation, it never covers everything, and for this reason it is thematically significant that the action of the novel overflows the parameters set by the structural metaphor. The arc of the rocket is the emblem of a paranoid vision of reality in which *"everything is connected"* in a way that contains history in a preordained pattern. At one point Tyrone Slothrop considers an alternative to this model of inflexible and eternal relations, "anti-paranoia, where nothing is connected to anything, a condition not many of us can bear for long" (p. 434). But this dichotomizing of the possibilities only shows how difficult it is for the synthesizing intellect to construe experience in any but absolute terms. Between the extremes of providential history and no history at all is secular history, where multiple connections of different sorts give meaning to experience without closing it down. The structural metaphor purports to contain the action of the novel by subordinating everything to what is literally a controlling theme. Because it eludes this control, the action stays in the realm of secular rather than providential history.

By providing a "structural" or "controlling" metaphor that falls short of structuring or controlling a novel that is radically uncentered and diffuse, Pynchon sets up a formal correlative for his lengthy and ebullient meditation on these two concepts, structure and control. As we have seen, he has been preoccupied with these concepts in all of his work. But in *Gravity's Rainbow*, he raises the issue in more general terms, so that in his most rigorously conceptual book, he addresses directly the premises behind any totalizing conceptual system. The fact that the encyclopedic novel aspires to the condition of such a system is consequently to the point. Pynchon exploits the assumptions of his chosen genre only to subvert them. In an important review, David Thorburn condemned the novel's "radically imperfect control of materials."[7] But Thorburn failed to observe that *Gravity's Rainbow* offers a vision of perfect control and then generates its energy—and its humor—from a refusal to pledge allegiance to that vision.

The following three sections of this chapter deal with the lure of totalizing structures in *Gravity's Rainbow* and the implications raised when such structures fail to control the narrative. The first section explores the multiple connotations that accrete to the "gravity's rainbow" of the title, making the rocket's arc a paradigm of "structures favoring death." The second section examines Pynchon's treatment of the structural metaphor in light of Murphy's law, the principle that denies authority to any theory purporting to explain everything. The third section considers some of the ways in which the text itself follows Murphy's law by eluding containment. Whereas the rocket, in Pynchon's evocative phrase, "is betrayed to Gravity," the text inverts this formula and betrays gravity—not only the gravity that should hold everything together but also the gravity that counsels high seriousness in the face of ultimate questions about structure and control. Because history is the preoccupation of this novel, these discussions dwell on the familiar project of giving history a definitive shape. In *Gravity's Rainbow* any world view that spatializes history implicitly invokes some version of the providential schema and denies real possibility. The alternative to a revisionist interpretation of the providential plan is secular history, which acknowledges the presence of multiple patterns in human affairs but recognizes the impossibility of reconciling these patterns in a single Authorized Version of reality. *Gravity's Rainbow* is in many ways a historical novel, but it is a novel about secular history.

"Structures Favoring Death"

In *V.* and *The Crying of Lot 49*, Pynchon seems fascinated by the apocalyptic implications of the linear narrative, and has exploited conventional expectations about development, complication, and resolution to expose the teleology latent in the assumption that experience somehow comes together as a story. His shadowy central figures V. and the Tristero personify history, and their inexorable development toward some ultimately nihilistic goal becomes an allegory for the inevitable decline of humanity—or at least becomes such an allegory for those characters (and readers) who are disposed to read experience as a plot. Both works parody the desire for narrative closure, a desire that presumes experience has meaning only when it is over and can be viewed in retrospect, from "outside," by presenting questing heroes who become so thoroughly implicated in the terms of their quests that there is no "outside" left for them. Both novels play variations on a central dilemma: if history has a meaningful order only when it is constituted as a linear narrative, it will make sense only after it has ended.

In *Gravity's Rainbow*, however, Pynchon gives spatial form to this implicitly apocalyptic construction of history and in this way exposes the embedded myth that history is a delusive veil over the eternal. The rainbow of the title is a historical trajectory, but it is also already present, "hanging there in the sky for everybody" (p. 490). Time is transmuted into space; like the path of the rocket as conceptualized by the Peenemünde engineers, processes "become architecture, and timeless" (p. 301). Both narrator and characters frequently employ the architectonic language of shape and pattern, and this rhetoric implies that an unchanging, comprehensive structure underlies all apparent novelty and that events in time only serve to complete or reveal this structure. Even the universal law of causation, the inflexible relation that turns the universe into a determined mechanism, reflects a partial and mistaken understanding of connections that in reality already exist— that is, can be perceived *sub specie aeternitatis*. As the ghost of Germany's assassinated foreign minister and industrialist Walter Rathenau reports from the Other Side, "All talk of cause and effect is secular history, and secular history is a diversionary tactic'' (p. 167).

Rathenau's specter (who of course must speak through a medium) is one of the many eccentric ''authorities'' that Pynchon brings in to testify about the ultimate dimensions of reality. But though such authorities are invariably suspect— they do appear under ambiguous circumstances and do tend to contradict one another—they cannot be written off: Pynchon refuses to establish a hierarchy among the cacophany of voices in *Gravity's Rainbow*. As the narrator remarks later on, human beings must try ''to make sense out of, to find the meanest sharp sliver of truth in so much replication, so much waste...'' (p. 590; Pynchon's ellipsis), and Rathenau claims to have the truth; in fact, he claims that it is possible ''to see the whole shape at once—'' (p. 165), which suggests that even time may be the delusion of creatures trapped within the providential schema. The ''shape'' of history is the same parabola that the rocket traces in its flight. In making this parabola the symbol of a totalizing vision of history, Pynchon compounds the implications of precisely the two questions that Rathenau raises: ''First, what is the real nature of synthesis? And then: what is the real nature of control?'' (p. 167). In *Gravity's Rainbow* synthesis and control are the hallmarks of ''structures favoring death.''

Rathenau's spirit offers these observations in the course of a séance convened by a group of Nazi officers and I.G. Farben executives. The assembly is interested in the future of the Farben monopoly, ''the growing, organic Kartell,'' as Rathenau sarcastically puts it, which has allowed the Third Reich to flourish and rearm for a global catastrophe.[8] For the German elite this monopoly is ''life'': life for the Reich, for the hydra-like corporation, and even for humanity, at least those parts of it that the Master Race has marked for Election. Rathenau sees it differently. The corporate structure is just another step toward crystallization of the entire planet:

The persistence, then, of structures favoring death. Death con- verted into more death. Perfecting its reign, just as the buried coal grows denser, and overlaid with more strata—epoch on top of epoch, city on top of ruined city. This is the sign of Death the impersonator. (P. 167)

All the productive energies of capitalism only guarantee the triumph of "structures favoring death." These structures persist, not because of some organic capacity to adapt, but because they are implicit in molecular organization. The history of polymerization, which has made the I.G. an inter- national cartel and given the Reich the economic power to make war—and rockets—has been in reality the unfolding of a cosmic plan to perfect death's reign over the earth. Rather than discovering new possibilities, technocrats are progres- sively revealing a pattern immanent in the nature of matter.

Rathenau claims that his perspective is privileged. He speaks from the standpoint of transcendence, and in this incident Pynchon makes it clear that such transcendence is inseparable from death. From the Other Side, death is reality and life is a sort of hallucination fostered by the aberrant vision of human beings trapped inside secular history. Ap- parent processes serve only to reveal a pattern that the dead can view *in toto*, and this pattern contains human history within an origin and an ending. From Rathenau's vantage, history aims to complete itself by approaching the pure, time- less state of the inorganic: "The real movement is not from death to any rebirth. It is from death to death-transfigured" (p. 166).

The central image of this preexisting pattern is, of course, the arc of the rocket. This arc suggests a life-span; the V-2 has "a life of its own," as Katje tells Slothrop (p. 301). As the story of the rocket's life, *Gravity's Rainbow* is the chronicle of a rise and fall. The book begins by describing an assortment of human machinations: the Allies' baroque propaganda schemes to frighten the Germans into surrendering; the I.G.'s attempts to enlist the aid of spirits to help control the international marketplace; Pointsman's efforts to plumb Slothrop's psyche for the key to his spontaneous erections. But there are already copious hints that human control is a delusion and that human actions succeed only when they conform to a sort of Hardyesque Immanent Will that technology has released from the earth. The rocket, Enzian tells Slothrop, has "a Destiny with a shape" (p. 362). When Slothrop eludes his observers and, following the track of this Destiny, reaches his personal *Brennschluss* in the Zone, his escape promises freedom. But after this midpoint Slothrop goes into a decline; he begins "to thin, to scatter" (p. 509), and the novel reflects this descent by fragmenting into shorter and less obviously related sections as it approaches its conclusion. The analogy is a system running down: a biological life losing cohesion as it nears its terminus; the universe gaining entropy as it makes the energy exchanges necessary to hold it together; providential history arriving at the decadence of its Last Days. Like Slothrop the rocket ascends on a "dream of escape," the dream of Mondaugen ("moon-eyes") and his colleagues at the Institute for Space Travel to leave the earth and in this rather literal-minded way to achieve transcendence. This dream is betrayed, not so much to malevolent human intentions as to the purpose latent in the V-2's technology.

Like *V.*, *Gravity's Rainbow* plays with the idea of a point in history where the weight of technology overcomes human purposes and takes its own path, leaving behind the inhabitants of an older organicist universe, whose only recourse becomes to construe techno-logic in terms of human ends and means. Characters as different as Katje, Blicero, the rocket-mystics at Peenemünde, and the Zone-Hereros accordingly interpret the rocket in religious terms and try to subsume their goals to its parody of will. One of Pynchon's satiric "sources," "*Tales of the Schwarzkommando*, collected by Steve Edelman," quotes Enzian as advising a white engineer, "'Proud man. . . . What are these data, if not direct revelation? Where have they come from, if not from the Rocket which is to be? How do you presume to compare a number you have only derived on paper with a number that is the Rocket's own?''' (p. 315). Behind this Zen-like pronouncement is a more traditionally Western model of religious significance. The rocket heralds what Slothrop's Puritan ancestors would have regarded as a new covenant, a new agreement between humanity and the omnipotent Hand that in the novel's closing hymn "turn [s] the time." In the language of covenant theology, the launching platform of the V-2 is "the axis of a particular Earth, a new dispensation, brought into being by the Great Firing" (p. 753).

In *Gravity's Rainbow* any comprehensive system for putting everything together is ultimately a variant on the Judeo-Christian myth because it appeals from a time-bound order to a transcendent perspective. The rainbow of the rocket's trajectory recalls the covenant between God and Noah in which God promised not to destroy the earth with water—an ironic bargain, as it turns out, because the rocket seems destined to destroy the earth with fire. This pact is the first of a succession of covenants that direct providential history to a preordained end and guarantee immortality to those whom God has chosen. The American Puritan twist on this theory was to accept the Calvinist doctrine that all events are absolutely predestined while stipulating that worldly success was the outward and visible sign that one had been chosen for salvation. America's Elect thus put God squarely behind their expanding cartels, claiming divine sanction for their own megalithic "structures favoring death."

In this way the Elect of the divine schema become the ruling elite called Them in *Gravity's Rainbow*, and Their revisionist reading of providential history appears to guarantee that the ruthless will inherit the earth. But by a further ironic twist, They too are swept up in the parabolic path of destiny and become unwitting victims of their own collaboration. Rathenau's preoccupation with the laws of matter signals the metamorphosis of theology into post-Newtonian metaphysics. The key term in this metamorphosis is "gravity": significantly, the rainbow of the title is not God's but gravity's. Newton arrived at the modern, deterministic understanding of cause and effect when he formulated his universal law of gravitation, and this law made the universe itself an Aggregät like the rocket, a self-propelling mechanism.[9]

The Encyclopedists abolished the redundant concept of God from the Newtonian system and announced that the only principle necessary to account for the integrity of the universe was gravity.[10] With the discovery of the second law of thermodynamics in the mid-nineteenth century, science both subsumed gravity to a higher principle and recovered a version of providential history by giving the clockwork universe a direction and a destination. The second law is frequently called Time's Arrow because it is the only physical precept that makes physical processes irreversible.[11] It gives the universe a *telos* in universal decay, dictating that higher forms of organization, the life forms, will be the first to disappear. In *Gravity's Rainbow* the rocket incorporates this promise of entropic dissolution and accelerates it. As the embodiment of Time's Arrow, the V-2 acts as both a totalizing principle and the principle dooming the totality to destruction. The unity of the system is its betrayal: a thermodynamically closed universe must run down, and the world of the novel is bounded by the rainbow, the track of a one-way trip. But in this version of providential history, there is no Election; no one will be saved. The new covenant betrays all previous covenants. The last paragraph of the novel places the last fall of the rocket in the absolute present while the narrator shifts to direct address.

> And it is just here, just at this dark and silent frame, that the pointed tip of the Rocket, falling nearly a mile per second, absolutely and forever without sound, reaches its last unmeasurable gap above the roof of this old theatre, the last delta-t.
> There is time, if you need the comfort, to touch the person next to you, or to reach between your own cold legs...(P. 760; Pynchon's ellipsis)

From the moment of its conception, the V-2 seemed destined to bring about a conflagration from which no one would escape.

The theme traced by the rocket's trajectory has to do with the way human beings have internalized and thus accelerated the universal entropic process by construing technology in human terms. For example, after acknowledging the superior force of the rocket, the Schwarzkommando decide to call it master. By serving the V-2 and ministering to its needs, they try to ally themselves with its destiny, a destiny that at first seems fragile and in need of protection. As Enzian tells Slothrop, "One reason we grew so close to the Rocket, I think, was this sharp awareness of how contingent, like ourselves, the Aggregat 4 could be—how at the mercy of small things . . ." (p. 362). The Schwarzkommando accordingly take the rocket as their Text and regard it as the coded testament of their people's fate. The rocket is to the Zone-Hereros as the Kabbala is to the Jews, and the capital "R" that Punchon bestows on the word "rocket" throughout suggests the extent to which this apparatus is personified by its beholders, or at least granted the ambiguous status of a totem.

Enzian's assessment of the rocket's contingency seems historically warranted, at least initially. Rocket development was also at the mercy of small things, not only the miscalculations and accidents that jeopardize any enormously complicated mechanism, but larger occasions of human irrationality. Because Hitler had a dream that the V-2 would never fly, the scientists at Peenemünde lost their funding for two years, an event that significantly retarded rocket development. Authorities from both sides have agreed that if the Führer had not treated his dream as prophecy, Germany might well have won the war.[12] But Enzian comes to suspect that such apparent setbacks are really diversionary tactics that both disguise and further the larger plan. As he rides through the ruins of a bombed oil refinery, "There doesn't exactly dawn, no but there *breaks*, as that light you're afraid will break some night at too deep an hour to explain away—there floods on Enzian

what seems to him an extraordinary understanding'' (p. 520).
With growing horror he begins to see the way that everything
might be connected in a pattern that transcends national
boundaries and humanly defined oppositions. The apparently
random devastations of the war suddenly appear to him as
necessary steps toward realizing a predetermined end.

> It means this War was never political at all, the politics was all
> theatre, all just to keep the people distracted...secretly, it was
> being dictated instead by the needs of technology...by a con-
> spiracy between human beings and techniques, by something that
> needed the energy-burst of war, crying, ''Money be damned, the
> very life of [insert name of Nation] is at stake,'' but meaning,
> most likely, *dawn is nearly here, I need my night's blood, my
> funding, funding, ahh more, more....* The real crises were crises
> of allocation and priority, not among firms—it was only staged to
> look that way—but among the different Technologies, Plastics,
> Electronics, Aircraft, and their needs which are understood only
> by the ruling elite... (P. 521; Pynchon's ellipses and brackets)

The Zone-Hereros' mistake was to view the rocket as an
isolated entity, one particular destiny among many. The real
Text is not a single Aggregät but the whole world reshaping
itself according to the mandates of technology. And these
mandates are prefigured in the composition of the earth itself.
"If you want the truth—I know I presume—" Rathnenau
counsels, "you must look into the technology of these
matters. Even into the hearts of certain molecules—it is they
after all which dictate temperatures, pressures, rates of flow,
costs, profits, the shapes of towers..." (p. 167; Pynchon's
ellipsis). From the world of the living, Enzian begins to
consider the possibility that the true sources of control lie
underneath the surface of an apparently accidental series of
scientific discoveries—that is, underneath the surface of an
apparently vital earth: "Up here, on the surface, coal-tars,
hydrogenation, synthesis were always phony, dummy functions to hide the real, *the planetary mission* yes perhaps
centuries in the unrolling...this ruinous plant, waiting for its

Kabbalists and new alchemists to discover the Key, teach the mysteries to others..." (p. 521; Pynchon's ellipses). But while this redefinition of the Text offers the Hereros a route In to the central fact of their own existence, it reduces them to impotent prophets. Like Byron the Bulb, they are "condemned to go on forever, knowing the truth and powerless to change anything" (p. 655). Their only solace is the knowledge that the pattern is universal, rendering distinctions between Elect and Preterite specious. Loyalty and obedience to Them is futile, for as Enzian tells Christian,

> They have lied to us. They can't keep us from dying, so They lie to us about death. A cooperative structure of lies. What have They ever given us in return for the trust, the love—They actually say 'love'—we're supposed to owe Them? Can They keep us from even catching cold? from lice, from being alone? from *anything*? Before the Rocket we went on believing, because we wanted to. But the Rocket can penetrate, from the sky, at any given point. Nowhere is safe. We can't believe Them any more. Not if we are still sane, and love the truth. (P. 728)

The truth releases the novel's Preterite from the task of serving and propitiating the ruling elite, but only because service and propitiation cannot alter the shape of fate.

Read in this way, *Gravity's Rainbow* itself resembles the Hereros' apocalyptic Text: certainly the information that Pynchon has assembled around the rocket's arc corroborates Rathenau's pronouncements and Enzian's paranoid vision. The novel incorporates most of the available information on the collaboration between German, American, British, and Dutch corporations throughout the war; "Don't forget," the narrator cautions, "the real business of the War is buying and selling" (p. 105); and again, "Secretly, [the War] was being dictated instead by the needs of technology" (p. 521). Enzian intuits a "mission," which Blicero designates later as the white man's real burden, "the mission to propagate death" that America has inherited from Europe (p. 722). The story of the rocket's rise and fall is the story of how America appropriated the Nazi *Vergeltungswaffen* and with them the Nazi bent toward annihilation. Blicero himself, the archetypal Aryan (his real name is Weissmann and his *nom de guerre* translates loosely as "bleacher"), has crossed the Atlantic, presumably with such members of the Elect as Dornberger and von Braun, to carry on the business of apocalypse. His Tarot concludes,

> If you're wondering where he's gone, look among the successful academics, the Presidential advisers, the token intellectuals who sit on boards of directors. He is almost surely there. Look high, not low.
>   His future card, the card of what will come, is The World. (P. 749)

As Raymond M. Olderman has observed, "*Gravity's Rainbow* is, at least in part, a history of Nazi consciousness and a demonstration of how that consciousness is potentially common to everyone."[13] Blicero is an avatar of that consciousness, and his entrenchment within the American hierarchy indicates how completely his White Death has infected America. But as Olderman suggests, Blicero is a symptom, not the source, of the disease. The device of the Tarot presumes a destiny already laid out. In the future the mission to propagate death will encompass the World.

The historical trajectory of the rocket takes it from its origins in the Berlin workshop of a group of space-struck amateurs to its transformation into the annihilating weapons of the present: the German V-2 is the direct ancestor of all current missile systems.[14] As Enzian suspected, the war was only one phase of the rocket's development. The V-2 could not become the delivery system for global catastrophe until it was combined with America's own contribution to the war effort, the atomic bomb. Blodgett Waxwing's report that "all the hepcats are going goofy over something called 'nuclear physics'" (p. 385), the nostalgia of Ensign Morituri (his name is Latin for "we who are about to die") for his home town, Hiroshima (p. 480), and Slothrop's discovery of a wirephoto showing "a giant white cock, dangling in the sky straight downward out of a white pubic bush" (p. 693) all ironically foreshadow the coming union between technologies. Coupled with the rocket's arc, the promise of nuclear catastrophe assumes the shape of inevitability. Gravity's rainbow gives geometrical form to the truism that what goes up must come down. In the rocket's beginning is its end. The temporal reversal that captures the imaginations of Pynchon's Londoners—the fact that the sound of the rocket's approach arrives after the explosion—only emphasizes the impossibility of escape. "Each firebloom, followed by blast then by sound of arrival, is a mockery (how can it not be deliberate?) of the reversible process" (p. 139), but reality is not reversible. The apparent distortion of sequence only underscores the fact that when a destiny is fixed, the events leading up to it merely articulate a pattern that is already there.

This destiny appears to guarantee that the world of *Gravity's Rainbow* is in decline; in terms of the rocket's arc, it is falling. But because it is imprisoned in a preordained historical trajectory, there is a familiar sense in which this world is already fallen—from Eden, from the innocence of its infancy, from the undifferentiated unity of the id—but always into time. The novel is pervaded by a rhetoric of nostalgia that takes the fact of history as a tragedy.[15] Time is a betrayal precisely because it is irreversible; each development brings humanity closer to the Final Zero, the end point at which death will have perfected its reign. On the most obvious level, the Fall introduces the vast sweep of providential history by plunging mankind into what Slothrop, invoking his Puritan forebears, calls "a sucking marshland of sin" (p. 364). But such "sin" has less to do with willed acts than with the experience of loss, and Pynchon supplements the traditional Christian imagery with historical, scientific, mythic, and mystical allusions to evoke a vision of the Fall as a flight from an original timeless center. This center is associated with "the infinitely dense point from which the present Universe expanded" (p. 396), but characters find the Fall so appealing as an explanatory structure that they adapt it to their own situations by locating a particular Eden in national or racial memory. For the anarchist Squalidozzi, "the Argentine heart, in its perversity and guilt, longs for a return to that first unscribbled serenity...that anarchic oneness of pampas and sky..." (p. 264; Pynchon's ellipses). Josef Ombindi, Enzian's rival among the Zone-Hereros, yearns for "an innocence he's really only heard about, can't himself believe in—the gathered purity of opposites, the village built like a mandala" of the tribal past, and "at times self-conned as any Christian, praises and prophesies that era of innocence he just missed living in, one of the last pockets of Pre-Christian Oneness left on the planet . . ." (p. 321). The original center was not only unity but a primal community, as Thomas Gwenhidway suggests when he equates history with the Diaspora: "What if we're all Jews, you see? all scattered like seeds? still flying outward from the primal fist so long ago"; and the narrator glosses, "He means alone and forever separate: Pointsman knows what he means" (p. 170). Attempts to recover this lost unity ironically ensure the triumph of "structures favoring death." The reverse of Gwenhidway's figure, "a Diaspora running backwards, seeds of exile flying inward in a modest preview of gravitational collapse, of the Messiah gathering in the fallen sparks" (p. 737), signals not a return to the beginning but an arrival at the end of history, and in context this anti-Diaspora is an ironic metaphor for the Fearful Assembly that gathers all of time into its end point.

In *Gravity's Rainbow* these multiple versions of the Fall provide a common origin for two important modernist images, the disintegrating center and the linear track of a history accelerating toward its own destruction. These images frequently converge, as in Slothrop's personal fall, which seems a variation on the Romanticist descent from the innocence of childhood. The arc of Slothrop's life begins with an original banishment by the Father; after his ascent to apparent freedom, his fate is to become "one plucked albatross. Plucked, hell—*stripped*. Scattered all over the Zone" (p. 712). This Fall also provides a genesis for the increased alienation of consciousness and the progressive framentation of understanding. In Geli Tripping's vision of "the World just before men," human consciousness is "that poor cripple, that deformed and doomed thing," which opposes a vitality "so clangorous and mad . . . that some spoiler *had* to be brought in before it blew the Creation apart" (p. 720). Consciousness here is both the repressive force of civilization and the isolating ego that cuts off instinctive urges within the psyche. Its weapon is Modern Analysis, which Blicero identifies with Original Sin (p. 722); and it is the analytic legacy that produces the two major methods of falsifying experience, "film and calculus, both pornographies of flight" (p. 567). Finally, this Fall is what has divorced words from an original coincidence with the things they stand for and has allowed language to proliferate, "dividing the Creation finer and finer, analyzing, setting namer more hopelessly apart from named, even to bringing in the mathematics of combination, tacking together established nouns to get new ones, the insanely, endlessly diddling play of a chemist whose molecules are words..." (p. 391; Pynchon's ellipses). The proliferation of words mimics the process by which chemists have taken molecules apart to produce new combinations— the process that produces "structures favoring death." The more luxuriant language grows, the further removed it is from original Presence. By this token alone, *Gravity's Rainbow* is a failed revelation, its explosions of language testifying to its inability to recover a primal unity.[16]

Like the history of the Hereros, the history of humanity as a whole is "one of lost messages" (p. 322). In its cosmic nostalgia, *Gravity's Rainbow* offers itself as a symptom of the irreversible process, proclaiming that the unifying, redemptive Word is irrevocably lost and that there is no going back. The manic proliferation of all aspects of human life affirms that the Center is gone, and that mankind can recover neither innocence nor divinity. And the most appalling thing about this Fall is that it is unmerited. People did not turn away from their gods; as Enzian reflects, "the gods had gone away themselves: the gods had left the people . . ." (p. 323). In terms of this myth of origins, secular history is an unwarranted punishment that places a whole planet "in bondage to falling" (p. 758) while masking the eternal shape of the real trajectory. In the absence of the gods, humanity is "at the mercy of a Gravity we have only begun to learn how to detect and measure" (p. 590). The only revelation that this gravity promises is that the world is destined for the grave.

Murphy's Law

As the preceding discussion indicates, a reading that encloses *Gravity's Rainbow* between its proposed myths of origin and ending makes the novel itself a structure favoring death. The book becomes a modernist theodicy, the twentieth century's epic response to that great Puritan epic *Paradise Lost*, asserting that there is no God but gravity and no way— or need—to justify the ways of gravity to men. The initial Fall, however it is construed, set history on a predetermined track. The tendency toward narrative fragmentation thus contributes to the structure, for the seemingly endless proliferation of human experience only shows how far secular history is from ideal unity.

"And yet, and yet:" the narrator interrupts when another system seems ready to close down definitively, "there is Murphy's Law to consider, that brash Irish proletarian restatement of Gödel's Theorem—*when everything has been taken care of, when nothing can go wrong, or even surprise us...something will*" (p. 275, Pynchon's ellipsis). "And yet, and yet," writes the science historian Jacob Bronowski, seizing on the same rhetoric in a strikingly similar context, "the laws of gravitation have gone. There is no gravitation;

there is no force at all; the whole model was wrong."[17] The history of science appears to confirm Murphy's law. Just as the post-Newtonian model of a clockwork universe—running because of gravity, running down because of entropy— seemed about to take care of everything, it fell apart. Or rather, it exploded under the pressure of the information it tried to contain.

Something similar happens to the rocket-centered cosmology of *Gravity's Rainbow*. This cosmology appears to arise from the combination of two images: an explosive Fall hurling shards of the Center infinitely outward, and a static, finite arc representing the track of postlapsarian history. Together, these images should produce the twentieth-century vision of apocalypse. But the two images do not really go together. The Fall results in a universe diversifying endlessly, out of control, abandoned by the gods. The arc is a metaphor for containment. The incompatibility of the two models attests to a failure of integration, where "to integrate," following the paradigm provided by rocket technology, "is to operate on a rate of change so that time falls away: change is stilled..." (p. 301, Pynchon's ellipsis). The Fall should provide a myth of origins for the eternal, determining parabola; it should be integrated to the immutable pattern of providential history. But in *Gravity's Rainbow* this explosive Fall becomes the explanation for another sort of tendency, the tendency of experience to diversify beyond prediction and control. And though the manic proliferation of events produces a terrifying vision of history, prediction and control are even more terrifying. A universe out of control is at least not committed to a determinate end. For this reason the Fall takes on the aspect of an extremely qualified *felix culpa*.

If the increasing multiplicity of experience indicates how far this experience is from primal unity, it also suggests that this experience may not ultimately cohere in structures favoring death. The case in point—and the test case for all totalizing structures within the novel—is the story of Tyrone Slothrop.

The problem that preoccupies the Pavlovian Dr. Pointsman, and later a number of other characters, is the nature of Slothrop's peculiar relation to the rocket. A map of London that Slothrop keeps in his office indicates that he always has his amorous adventures in places that V-2s subsequently hit, and this initial piece of data leads Pointsman to postulate a cause-and-effect relationship between Slothrop's erections and rocket explosions. Slothrop must be responding to some aspect of the V-2, and his affinity for this apparatus must have its source in some childhood incident: Pointsman's thesis is so much a part of ordinary psychologistic notions of character development that at first it seems self-evident, so that even the Pavlovian trappings of his explanation do not signal that this explanation is overly reductive. Slothrop is famous in psychology textbooks as Infant Tyrone, the first human subject of an experiment in operant conditioning. And so the project of explaining Slothrop, which for the reader is also the project of "understanding" Slothrop's character, centers on attempts to identify the original stimulus used to produce Slothrop's infant erections.

The book duly produces this stimulus, a synthetic known as Imipolex G. But this identification does not resolve the mystery of Slothrop's own identity for several reasons. First of all, Slothrop has his erections on V-2 targets before the V-2s are even launched. If there is a causal link between phallic character and phallic rocket, the rocket should be responding to Slothrop, rather than vice versa. Second, Imipolex-G is not standard V-2 hardware; it is incorporated into only one rocket, the rocket that carries Gottfried as its payload. The Mystery Stimulus has no connection with the distribution of targets, and it is this distribution that the stimulus-response theory attempts to explain. Third, and most important, it turns out that Slothrop has falsified much of the information on his map (pp. 271, 302), so that Pointsman has to hypothesize, finally, that Slothrop's fantasies, not Slothrop's behavior, need explaining (p. 272). At this point Pointsman's project of enclosing Slothrop in a "labyrinth of conditioned-reflex work" (p. 88) seems doomed, as Slothrop's affinity with the V-2 recedes into a pattern of appallingly "Kute Korrespondences."

But the correspondences are so intrusive that they suggest a more occult connection underlying surface similarities. As Rathenau insinuated, causal explanations may fail only because they remain partial, reflecting an inability to see "the whole shape at once." As a personified penis (for his erections are his defining feature, at least initially), Slothrop resembles both the rocket and Imipolex G, "the first plastic that is actually *erectile*" (p. 699). In some cosmic equation, it seems that Slothrop *is* both Aggregät and synthetic, and the erotic impulse that links him to these inanimate Doubles appears to commit him to reenacting their destiny.

The larger question thus becomes whether Slothrop's life will recapitulate the "life" of the rocket—whether he will serve as a microcosm of a universal pattern within *Gravity's Rainbow*. And it is possible to construe his story in terms of the parabolic trajectory. Slothrop's "launch" occurs in his infancy, when he is conditioned to respond with an erection to a chemical stimulus. Like the rocket he "ascends" under guidance, provided first by Laszlo Jamf's emissaries in America and later by Pointsman and certain of his colleagues at The White Visitation. When Pointsman allows him to escape into the Zone, Slothrop metaphorically reaches *Brennschluss*, the midpoint of his flight path at which control is deliberately terminated. At this point Slothrop believes he is about to discover the truth about his situation, and conventional wisdom would suggest that self-knowledge will allow him to take responsibility for his own destiny. Ironically, it is self-knowledge that seems to shatter him, leaving him free only to fall. He eludes Their control only to be betrayed to gravity; as his story continues, his personality becomes more and more diffused as he loses his ability to keep information together.[18] This "descent" brings his trajectory into conjunction with the fragmenting Fall and affirms that dreams of escape and autonomy are delusions. In this way Slothrop's decline becomes an allegory for the tendency of things to fall apart as civilization accelerates the universal entropic process.

But this reading of the Slothrop story passes over the ambiguities of Slothrop's dénouement—passes them over rather as the Calvinist God ''passes over'' the Preterite of his providential scheme, condemning them to an inconsequence that is finally damnation. In the last two chapters of *Gravity's Rainbow*, Pynchon uses a number of strategies to insist that this godlike perspective on the action is not an option for the reader. In particular he makes it impossible to explain even what happens to Slothrop by making Slothrop elude containment. When Slothrop enters the ''descent'' phase of his trajectory, he loses his mysterious resemblance to the rocket—although not through any plan or exercise of will—first by diversifying his supposedly determined sexual behavior and later by diversifying his whole personality to the point where he is no longer available for study. As a consequence, he escapes the rocket's destiny, although his own destiny remains not only uncertain but in a sense inconceivable. By the end of the novel, Slothrop has lost his identity; he is no longer a unified character. However unsettling this outcome may be, one implication is that he has escaped control, for it is his phallocentric identity that has ''placed'' him in the apocalyptic pattern. By fragmenting beyond containment, Slothrop ceases to be what the political philosopher Herbert Marcuse calls a one-dimensional man, wholly defined by his technologized society. He becomes instead the hyperbolic embodiment of many-dimensional man, decentralized beyond control, beyond containment, and so in the root sense beyond comprehension.[19]

If Slothrop is initially defined synecdochically by reference to one portion of his anatomy, this aspect of his body and his behavior becomes progressively less important as he moves through the Zone. He explodes into polymorphous perversity, and his final sexual performance before he loses coherence as a character opens up new vistas for pornography by introducing a previously unknown unnatural act that might reasonably be called a nose job.

> . . . Trudi is kissing him into an amazing comfort, it's an open house here, no favored senses or organs, all are equally at play ...for possibly the first time in his life Slothrop does not feel obliged to have a hardon, which is just as well, because it does not seem to be happening with his penis so much as with...oh mercy, this is embarrassing but...well his *nose* actually seems to be erecting, the mucus beginning to flow yes a nasal hardon here and Trudi has certainly noticed all right, how could she help but...
> (P. 439, Pynchon's ellipses)

This incident marks the decentralization of Slothrop's sexuality; he is degenitalized, after a fashion, although it is not the fashion Pointsman has in mind when he orders Slothrop's castration. Slothrop escapes this castration by the simple expedient of exchanging clothes with the phallocentric character Major Marvy, for by this time only his garments identify him. With the diffusion of his sexuality, his identity has become so unstable that as the narrator comments, "It's doubtful if he can ever be 'found' again, in the conventional sense of 'positively identified and detained'" (p. 712). He becomes radically uncentered, a fate that brings him to the opposite extreme of his initial characterization as a personified penis. Near the conclusion the narrator describes Bodine

> looking straight at Slothrop (being one of the few who can still see Slothrop as any sort of integral creature any more. Most of the others gave up long ago trying to hold him together, even as a concept—"It's just got too remote"'s what they usually say).
> (P. 740)

It is possible to naturalize the idea that Slothrop "thins" and "scatters" (p. 509)—for instance, by regarding Slothrop's dissolution as psychic breakdown, amnesia, or death. But all such attempts to enclose Slothrop in an explanatory structure (which tacitly affirm Pointsman's working premises by making Slothrop an object of study) fail to comprehend him, "even as a concept." Slothrop's conceptual fragmentation becomes an emblem for the impossibility of explaining him—which is also the impossibility of explaining him away. As a decentralized presence, Slothrop cannot be dismissed. He saturates the last part of the novel: as a topic of rumor and conjecture; as a type of the Fool, the Rilkean Angel, Orpheus, and Christ; as Byron the Bulb, a rock kazooist, the harmonicist named Adenoid, and the hero of a number of surrealistic flashbacks to his childhood and adolescence; and as a sporadic infuence on the narrative voice: "Fine crew this is, getting set to go off after the Radiant—say what? what's Slothrop's *own* gift and Fatal Flaw? Aw, *c'mon*—" (p. 676). By giving Slothrop this peculiar omnipresence, Pynchon thwarts his characters' desire to encapsulate Slothrop in an explanatory structure and in this way to transcend him.

This point is important because in *Gravity's Rainbow* the desire to objectify experience as a conceptual totality is always the desire to transcend the merely human. Synthesis and control are interrelated, as Rathenau insinuated, and all the processes of putting things together in this novel—from polymerization to rocket assembly to international monopolies—are ways by which people try to unite phenomena in a closed system that leaves them outside, allied with the malign manipulators of providential history. The shadowy force known as Them is by definition outside the secular realm of human actions, sometimes so far outside that They seem to operate from the Other Side of life, the world of the dead. The search for control is an attempt to attain Their perspective on the action and in this way to transcend secular history.

But the project of transcendence raises insuperable problems about the whole notion of "outside." "They" is always the name given to the detached, manipulative Others, but perceptions of just who They are vary depending on the position of the perceiver. Sometimes They are simply authoritative figures: the Elect of the Puritan church, political leaders, corporate executives, even parents. But members of such elite groups derive their authority from higher and more removed sources: the Elect from the finally inscrutable will of their God; the political figures from their corporate bankrollers; these corporate heads from their products, which in turn depend on the internal configurations of matter; parents from *their* parents, trapped in a patriarchal system where, Blicero tells Gottfried, "Fathers are carriers of the virus of Death, and sons are the infected" (p. 723). By attempting to get outside a controlling system, such authoritative figures only confirm that there is a more comprehensive system controlling them.

The problem with such secular power is that it is not absolute; it does not allow its wielders to transcend the human condition, which as the resolution of the Counterforce's Gross Suckling Conference proclaims, is "at the mercy of death and time" (p. 706). In *Gravity's Rainbow* the lure of transcendence is its promise of immortality. And so Blicero tells Gottfried, "I want to break out—to leave this cycle of infection and death. I want to be taken in love: so taken that you and I, and death, and life, will be gathered, inseparable, into the radiance of what we would become . . ." (p. 724). Ironically, human beings transcend mortality only by choosing death. But Blicero's statement is not a preface to his suicide. Instead, it introduces what the novel presents as the archetypal displacement of the death wish, the sacrifice of the son.[20] By constricting, oppressing, and finally killing others, people try to rise above their common humanity and to ensure their own immortality. And as Rathenau tells the leaders of the Reich, such attempts really assure the triumph of death over all of life.

Rathenau's ambiguous presence at the séance, however, is one of many indications that death is not precisely the same as annihilation in the world of the novel. As the Wernher von Braun headnote suggests, a great deal points to "the continuity of our spiritual existence after death." Voices from the Other Side haunt the narrative, combined at times with hints that the real They operate from a sphere where history is already finished and time is only a record of moves that have been made for all eternity. For example, when Slothrop stumbles into the gaming room of the Casino Hermann Goering, he has a premonition: "The odds They played here belonged to the past, the past only. Their odds were never probabilities, but frequences *already observed*" (p. 208). But even at this exalted level of transcendence, such a They-system is not omnipotent. "There are times when Slothrop actually can find a clutch mechanism between him and Their iron-cased engine far away up a power train whose shape and design he has to guess at, a clutch he can disengage . . ." (p. 207). No matter how removed They seem, They are never so completely outside as to be beyond reach. They are suscep-tible to tampering.

For this reason the notion of transcendence becomes strangely equivocal in *Gravity's Rainbow*. In a note at the beginning of the novel, von Braun argues for spiritual con-tinuity on the basis of empirical procedures: "Nature does not know extinction; all it knows is transformation. Everything science has taught me, and continues to teach me, strengthens my belief in the continuity of our spiritual existence after death." His reasoning involves a curious leap from the con-servation of matter to some hitherto unknown scientific principle dealing with the conservation of spirit, and this leap suggests that von Braun simply assumes that spirit, whatever it is, is part and parcel of that same natural order that science claims as its object of study. Spiritual existence thus makes itself at home in the natural world and displays characteristic, if eccentric, behavior. In the novel the staff of The White Visitation are dedicated to the study of this behavior and seem to live cheek-by-jowl with disembodied beings who are in many ways more contingent and fragile than the humans sur-rounding them. Late in the narrative, a number of the in-habitants of the Other Side join the Counterforce and help this group subvert the secular Establishment. Even Rathenau, who claims that from his vantage "it's possible to see the whole shape at once," has to come when he is called and must relay his elliptical insights to a human audience. In all these ways, the novel domesticates the idea of transcendence. If the Other Side confers special powers, such powers always have limits, so that spirits remain actively involved in history, like Olympian gods rather than the Judeo-Christian God of Creation. Such spirits are not ultimately detached and do not have ultimate control. They are simply inhabitants of the Other Side—the flip side of a single system, this name implies. The true They ought to transcend the system entirely.

By offering this motley collection of spirits as representatives of the superhuman, Pynchon parodies attempts to imagine a completely transcendent They-system. To make transcendence intelligible is to make it immanent. They become rather like us, and open to our interference. In *Gravity's Rainbow* characters on every level of the social and political hierarchy intuit a larger pattern that renders them impotent. Paranoia becomes a configuration like a Chinese puzzle, where every system of control turns into evidence for a more encompassing system. But it is theoretically impossible for these internal syntheses to take their places once and for all in the culminating pattern—theoretically impossible according to Murphy's law, which Pynchon makes the ontological equivalent of Gödel's theorem.

Gödel's theorem says that no logical system can be complete. Such a system always depends for its coherence on axioms that remain "outside" the system because they are unprovable within the system. A more comprehensive system that encompasses these hitherto "outside" axioms must rest on further axioms that it cannot prove, and so on. There can be no set of all sets, no completely comprehensive logical system, because no logical system can account for all the principles that guarantee its own coherence.[21] In this sense even logical structures depend on outside control.

By making Murphy's law a "brash Irish proletarian restatement of Gödel's Theorem," Pynchon implies that a truism of experience—something will go wrong, something will always surprise us—derives from the necessary incompleteness of all totalizing conceptual systems. Such systems purport to account for everything that exists; for this reason they are always They-systems, contingent on an outside power that guarantees their coherence. But if They actually exist, They belong inside the system that purports to account for everything that exists. The system must be enlarged to encompass Them, and in the process it becomes another system, with other controlling principles. If They are really outside the system, They cannot exist; They recede to the status of either operational principles or hallucinations, depending on the paranoia of the perceiver. Though there are any number of possible systems involving any number of groups that can be called "Them," none of these systems can be definitive and no They can have absolute control. There is always room for surprises.[22]

In *Gravity's Rainbow* They-systems arise when people try to become Them by objectifying the world of experience as a conceptual totality. In looking for the cause of Slothrop's erections, for instance, Pointsman tries to prove "the stone determinacy of everything, of every soul. There will be precious little room for any hope at all. You can see how important a discovery like that would be" (p. 86). Ironically, Pointsman can "see" everything about his thesis except the fact that it will prove his own determination. His "labyrinth of conditioned-reflex work" appears a route to transcendence, and he cannot imagine himself occupying any stance but that of the privileged observer who studies the absurdly predictable behavior of humanity with the detachment of a clinician. It is only late in his career that Pointsman begins to grasp the full implications of his work, and then he has to posit Their omnipotence as a necessary condition of his system: "They own everything: Ariadne, the Minotaur, even, Pointsman fears, himself" (p. 88). In erecting a comprehensive explanatory structure, Pointsman has been working to prove he is in Their maze.

Franz Pökler is another scientist who gets caught in his own labyrinth. Unlike Pointsman, Pökler is aware that he is being manipulated by external powers; but he chooses to collaborate with this manipulation, to the point of offering himself as victim to his sadistic commanding officer Weissmann/Blicero, in the hopes that he will be allowed the role of a domesticated Dr. Mabuse in the coming technologized state. Seduced by the vision of a higher totality that links the emerging rocket to fate, Pökler denies the human relations that connect him to his family by accepting without question Blicero's bureaucratic parody of a daughter, an "Ilse" who comes to him in cinematic "frames" and who may or may not be the same girl from one summer to the next. It is only when he learns that both his wife and daughter have been confined in the concentration camp he passes every day that Pökler realizes how thoroughly he has been ensnared in the network of official lies dictating that human beings are replaceable components. He has refused to acknowledge the reality that has been before him all the time because he has allowed himself to see only the architectonic purity of a rocket-centered cosmology. "If he must curse Weissmann, then he must also curse himself. Weissmann's cruelty was no less resourceful than Pökler's own engineering skill, the gift of Daedelus that allowed him to put as much labyrinth as required between himself and the inconveniences of caring" (p. 428).

Pökler's engineering skill allows him to replace concern with allegiance to a cosmic plan in the process of unfolding: "It was impossible not to think of the Rocket without thinking of *Shicksal*, of growing toward a shape predestined and perhaps a little otherworldly" (p. 416). In effect, Pökler has obeyed the injunction of his old teacher, the same Dr. Jamf who performed the conditioned-reflex experiment on Slothrop. Jamf counseled renunciation of the fragile covalent bond that is the basis of life structures, in favor of the stronger ionic bond that assures the relative permanence of inanimate structures. For Jamf the ionic bond becomes the symbol of a whole metaphysics, and in *Gravity's Rainbow* this metaphysics underlies all attempts to totalize experience in an immutable conceptual system.

> In the last third of his life, there came over Lazslo Jamf—so it seemed to those who from out of the wood lecture halls watched his eyelids slowly granulate, spots and wrinkles grow across his image, disintegrating it toward old age—a hostility, a strangely *personal* hatred, for the covalent bond. A conviction that, for synthetics to have a future at all, the bond must be improved on—some students even read "transcended." That something so mutable, so *soft*, as a sharing of electrons by atoms of carbon should be at the core of life, *his* life, struck Jamf as a cosmic humiliation. *Sharing*? How much stronger, how everlasting was the *ionic* bond—where electrons are not shared but *captured*. *Seized*! and held! polarized plus and minus, these atoms, no ambiguities...how he came to love that clarity: how stable it was, such mineral stubbornness! (P. 577, Pynchon's ellipsis)

Jamf's rhetoric of capturing and seizing foreshadows the absolutist rhetoric of the Third Reich—the "lion in each one of you" who champions the ionic bond "takes, he holds! He is not a Bolshevik or a Jew. You will never hear relativity from the lion. He wants the absolute" (p. 577)—but in rejecting transient and unstable connections, Jamf also articulates the assumptions behind any system that purports to explain everything once and for all. Such a system is built on the premise that eternal relations alone are real. The varied and unpredictable manifestations of life can only be negligible particulars that accumulate in accordance with a general law. In aiming to do away with life altogether, Jamf merely underscores the tendency of such systems to relegate the imprecisions of lived experience to a subsidiary status. His reasoning is palpably insane: it is as a living human being that he proposes to exalt the inanimate over the living. But this insanity is exceptional in the novel only because it acknowledges the obvious. Totalizing conceptual structures invariably damn the consciousness that creates them in *Gravity's Rainbow*. And in their efforts to make such structures into realities, theorists like Jamf reify their nihilistic premises in totalitarian systems.

For this reason the "structures favoring death" are real without being absolute or inescapable. They are real because people make them, in an effort to make total sense out of their situations. But because people make them, these structures never reflect some ultimate truth about the universe. They are not imposed from outside by a conjectural Them who can stand aloof from historical processes. In *Gravity's Rainbow* there is always a Pogo-like sense in which They are Us, a fact that is not necessarily consoling but that does present some room for unanticipated developments. Because no one ever succeeds in getting "outside" human experience, no one has the key that explains everything. Despite the persuasiveness of totalizing models of reality, there is no "outside" and no key. It is impossible to account for everything that happens. In fact, it is impossible even to account for what happens to Slothrop.

The project of accounting for Slothrop is central in the novel precisely because Slothrop's affinity with the rocket promises to make him a mirror of all the forces at work in the cosmos. "We were never that concerned with Slothrop *qua* Slothrop," reports a member of the Counterforce in an interview with the house organ of Them, the *Wall Street Journal*. "Some called him a 'pretext.' Other felt that he was a genuine, point-for-point microcosm" (p. 738). The academic tone is unsettling: the early Counterforce had regarded Slothrop as a member of their insurgent We-system, "a good guy after all" (p. 619). By substituting concepts like "pretext" and "microcosm" for such characteristically human bonds as concern, loyalty, and friendship, this unidentified spokesman appears to be reverting to Pointsman's stance. Slothrop is once again an object for study. But it is in this passage that Pynchon makes his most poignant case for the universality of Pointsman's stance. The desire to transcend and explain away the facts of experience is not limited to professional scientists; it is fundamental to consciousness. Yet this desire is also a betrayal. To objectify experience as a conceptual unity is to "go over" to the side of the antihuman and the gods, to side against life. And so the Counterforce representative interpolates a strangely intimate admission into his testimony: "[. . . I am betraying them all...the worst of it is I know what your editors want, *exactly* what they want. I am a traitor. I carry it with me. Your virus . . .]" (p. 739). Like Pökler the speaker collaborates knowingly in a betrayal that is finally his own betrayal, by making experience into a conceptually closed system. Such a system is "what your editors want—*exactly* what they want," not only the editors of the *Wall Street Journal* but the editors at the Viking Press, which published *Gravity's Rainbow*. In this way Pynchon insists that not even he is immune to "your virus," the need to contain and explain away ongoing processes.[23] This need infects the text as a desire to achieve resolution; by analogy it infects history as the desire to achieve a definitive shape. The image of the rocket poised "above the roof of this old theatre" on the last page emphasizes the imminent possibility of a conclusion that will leave the reader outside the novel, transcending its concerns, free to write off *Gravity's Rainbow* as a self-contained system.

In this way *Gravity's Rainbow* capitalizes on the tension between fidelity to the secular realm of human actions and the drive to unify and be as gods, gods who turn out to be the malign manipulators of providential history. The persistent irony is that human beings are never allowed to transcend their condition: the hyperbolically inclusive description of the rocket's final descent implies that to close the action is to annihilate even the reader. The impulse to provide conceptual unity traps consciousness in its own labyrinth. For this reason it is thematically significant that the novel, like Slothrop, is difficult to hold together, even as a concept.

The concept is there, of course. It is intrusively present in the form of a structural metaphor that constitutes a ready-made overview. But the arc of the V-2 controls the action only to the extent that things are more important than people and ideas are more important than things. If the parabola shapes the novel, the central character is the rocket, and human actions are only accessories to what the narrator at one point calls the Fearful Assembly (p. 738). Virtually all the major characters are haunted by this reading of their experience, and consequently their various interpretations of the rocket's mission and message condition their understanding of their own situations. But the reader who makes the rocket the conceptual center of the book is ironically forced to pass over what is most engaging and moving and, like Philip Morrison, who wrote the important review for *Scientific American*, may conclude that *Gravity's Rainbow* is "a brilliant book, but . . . that glow is icy cold."[24]

By yielding to the lure of totality and "passing over" recalcitrant elements that refuse to conform to the novel's parody of an overarching structural metaphor, such a reader unwittingly aligns himself with the Calvinist God, who damns the preterite aspects of his creation. But the text claims that preterition can be a kind of grace. As Slothrop's heretical ancestor William suggested, the things that do not fit may be the most important because they bear witness to the inability of the providential schema to account for everything (p. 555). The Hereros express this inversion with what Enzian calls "a mantra for times that threaten to be bad. . . . Mba-kayere. It means 'I am passed over'" (p. 362).[25] In *Gravity's Rainbow* to be passed over is a condition for survival and thus a basis for hope.

For as there is no transcendent God behind the apocalyptic schema, man has had to invent him; or rather, this God is the invention of "The Man [who] has a branch office in each of our brains, his corporate emblem is a white albatross, each local rep has a cover known as the Ego, and their mission is Bad Shit" (pp. 712–13). So far, the text suggests, the Preterite

have been all too willing to collaborate in their own destruction; they represent "the lemming point of view" (p. 554). But
even lemmings are not bound by some inflexible Nature of
Things. Ludwig's pet lemming Ursula somehow circumvents
the Man in her brain and returns to her owner, inexplicably
violating the pattern established for her species. Humanity
appears to be in a similarly anomalous position, committed to
nihilistic systems but unable to close these systems and thus
to rule out rude intrusions into an apparently fixed destiny.
Pynchon's proposed dirge for the race is "Sold on Suicide," a
song that catalogues the alternatives to annihilation in order to
reject them one by one and ends up serving as a dubious
affirmation of life simply because it is logically impossible to
reject every aspect of it:

> In its complete version it represents a pretty fair renunciation of
> the things of the world. The trouble with it is that by Gödel's
> Theorem there is bound to be some item around that one has
> omitted from the list, and such an item is not easy to think of off
> the top of one's head, so that what one does most likely is go back
> over the whole thing, meantime correcting mistakes and inevita-
> ble repetitions, and putting in new items that will surely have
> occurred to one, and—well, it's easy to see that the "suicide" of
> the title might have to be postponed indefinitely! (p. 320)

If there are reasons for optimism in *Gravity's Rainbow*,
Pynchon does not ground them in anything like human dignity
or man's indomitable will. Both dignity and will conspire to set
history on an annihilating trajectory. In their commitment to
control over their own destinies, people appear irrevocably
sold on suicide. The mitigating factor is that complete control
is impossible. Something always goes wrong. Spectacular
vaults into Nothingness turn into pratfalls; for all the death-
ward tendency of the action, not one of the major characters
dies. The Komikal Kamikazes (who violate the closing chapter without introduction, warning, or explanation) express this
general state of affairs in a remarkably unenigmatic haiku,

The lover leaps in the *volcano*!
It's ten feet deep,
And inactive—   (P. 691)

By providing the convenient handle of the structural metaphor, Pynchon duplicitously invites his readers to seize on an
apocalyptic reading and in this way to confirm that humanity
is eager to collaborate in its own betrayal. Like the rocket,
such readers are betrayed to gravity. As the conclusion emphasizes, they cannot transcend the unifying structure that
they have affirmed and can only wait for annihilation—as even
They must wait. But a reading guided by the structural metaphor passes over far too much, and in particular it subordinates or simply ignores most of the humor of an extraordinarily funny novel. This humor has nothing to do with divine
comedy or abstract programs of salvation. It always arises
from violations of an apparent order: from liberating, if
generally unnerving, surprises. And this observation may be
the most compelling argument against a totalizing, Procrus-
tean reading of *Gravity's Rainbow*. To take the arc of the
rainbow seriously as a controlling metaphor is to betray a
richly comic novel to the excessive gravity of its providential
plot.

Narrative Theory and Practice

In its extreme decentralization, *Gravity's Rainbow* offers
itself as secular rather than providential history. It mirrors a
world characterized by uncontrollable proliferation, and if this
world is fallen because it has no center, the Fall is less a primal
tragedy than a cosmogonic myth for what is finally a comic
state of affairs. Experience does not confine itself to working
out the apocalyptic pattern; it spreads out in unanticipated
directions, defying expectations and eluding containment.
And the text of *Gravity's Rainbow* explodes into complexity,
even as it purports to yearn after an ideal simplicity. It is this

incredible complexity that makes the novel so funny, or so irritating, depending on the reader's commitment to totalizing structures. Opinion has been divided since the Pulitzer Advisory Board clashed with the Editorial Board over whether to award Pynchon the 1973 prize for fiction, and the more orthodox Advisory Board's charges that the novel was "unreadable," "turgid," and "overwritten" suggest the degree to which the novel violates both metaphysical and aesthetic expectations of wholeness.[26] Thematically, the novel challenges the commonsense dictum that experience illustrates general truths about a unitary and at least theoretically comprehensible universe. Structurally it challenges one of the most embedded assumptions of literary orthodoxy, that any novel is at root a coherence system, introducing formal innovations only within a controlling convention so that surprises, when properly understood, cease to be surprising. In both enterprises Pynchon opposes inevitability.

The action of the novel occupies the space that Frank Kermode, borrowing the language of religious apocalyptic, calls "in the middest," between myths of origin and myths of ending.[27] If *Gravity's Rainbow* were committed to some modernist version of providential history, these two myths would take precedence, and the period in which the action takes place would emerge at the conclusion as a representative slice of the historical trajectory. The years 1944–45 would be important insofar as they illustrated a universal tendency or movement, and in the context of the multiple versions of apocalypse, this movement would be toward annihilation. Like the rocket a world bound to the eternal parabola hurtles "kingdom-of-deathward." If the novel intends to embrace a preordained pattern, everything in it should point to this conclusion.

Of course, not everything points to this conclusion. "*Everything* is some kind of a plot, man," Bodine tells Slothrop; and Leni, still disguised as the prostitute Solange, adds, "And yes but, the arrows are pointing all different ways," demonstrating with "a dance of hands, red-pointed fingervectors" (p. 603). The narrative appears to follow Leni's gesture, shooting off in different directions and fostering often contradictory tendencies. In effect, Leni's gesture dramatizes the Preterite vision of reality, which is the view from inside, "in the middest." The idea of a coherent pattern that reconciles all these divergent movements assumes the existence of a privileged perspective outside history. If such a perspective is impossible, the single plot does not exist.

Gravity's Rainbow denies the existence of a single plot by refusing to take a transcendent perspective on the action. Not only the characters are "in the middest"; the narrator also speaks from inside history, in the present tense. The effect is to give immediacy to actions that, somewhat paradoxically, take place in a recognizable segment of the past. *Gravity's Rainbow* is a historical novel; it is so thoroughly "period," in fact, that it appears obsessive in its amassing of detail. But it is a historical novel about secular history, about the inside view of an irreducibly plural reality, and for this reason it does not claim the usual historical privilege of hindsight. In retrospect, history takes its place on the time-line; it becomes linear inasmuch as it is teleological, a being-toward the present. Pynchon throws the dubious advantage of such hindsight into question by presenting history as a continual present and dwelling on the minutiae of his chosen period as if they constituted immediate surroundings. One consequence is that these details are not organized in a rigid hierarchy of significance. The Preterite point of view lacks a consistent principle of subordination simply because it is the view from inside. The outside perspective, looking back on events, can make hard-and-fast distinctions between important and trivial facts, but this is because this outside perspective implicitly translates time into space. To historicize is to give shape to history, the shape of necessity insofar as things happen as a consequence of some preceding event. The working-out of history, construed in terms of antecedents and consequents, becomes a progressive closing down of possibilities as each development restricts future options. As the pluralistic world recedes into the past, it becomes imperceptibly a world where invisible forces carry out the demands of destiny. The outside perspective fits secular history into some version of the providential pattern. Pynchon distrusts this outside perspective because it is never truly outside—it is only the stance of human beings who deny their own involvement in history in a pathetic attempt to emulate Their hypothesized transcendence. By adopting a present-tense mode of narration, he can treat the past as a present that was. From inside, history has any number of shapes, or plots pointing in all directions, which is to say that when the subject is secular history, there are no Authorized Versions.

Because secular history can invoke no single principle of subordination, the historical minutiae of the novel multiply; in the language of Murphy's law, they "spontaneously generate" (p. 275) more facts, more revelations, more implications, and more perspectives. The long catalogues, for instance, revel in a democracy of detail. Slothrop is introduced through an inventory of his desk top, which is layered with the debris of his bureaucratic life like the layers of earth that Rathenau reports lying over the "preterite dung" of the coal-tars, with the difference that the hierarchy of layers is not significant in Slothrop's case; the "base of bureaucratic smegma" made up of "millions of tiny red and brown curls of rubber eraser, pencil shavings, dried tea or coffee stains, traces of sugar and Household Milk, much cigarette ash, very fine black debris picked and flung from typewriter ribbons, decomposing library paste, broken aspirins ground to powder" is no more characteristic than subsequent layers containing "an empty Kreml hair tonic bottle, lost pieces to different jigsaw puzzles showing parts of the amber left eye of a Weimaraner, the green velvet folds of a gown, slate-blue veining in a distant cloud, the orange nimbus of an explosion (perhaps a sunset), rivets in the skin of a Flying Fortress, the pink inner thigh of a pouting pin-up girl...a few old Weekly Intelligence Summaries from G-2, a busted corkscrewing ukelele string," and so on (p. 18; Pynchon's ellipsis). This description builds up a revealing picture of Slothrop and of the wartime British atmosphere surrounding him, suggesting the ways in which Slothrop himself is a jumbled composite of tastes and tendencies, always open to new accretions. This introduction to the character is important because it works against the theory of Pointsman and his fellow psychologists that Slothrop is a kind of hierarchical system made up of levels, and that there is an underlying *Ur*-Slothrop who can be identified with a conditioned reflex. Slothrop's multiple defining characteristics coexist in a messily egalitarian state, a situation that suggests it may not be possible to predict what will be his "controlling" feature from one moment to the next.

Sometimes the catalogues deal explicitly with the project of trying to exhaust a set of period details. One of the funniest episodes in the book explores the culture shock of the G.I. confronted with the inexplicable British penchant for "wine jellies" ("The English are kind of weird when it comes to the way things taste, Mom," Slothrop writes home [p. 116], summing up a discovery made by countless American servicemen stationed in England); and the humor of the passage stems largely from the fact that it goes on and on, taking Slothrop through variation after noxious variation on the innocent-looking candy with the "unspeakably awful" surprise filling (pp. 115–19). A more sober catalogue later in the book lists the displaced Nationalities who move through the Zone in "a great frontierless streaming" (p. 549), and this catalogue is so packed with sensuously evoked historical detail that it too promises to go on indefinitely. The details present a painstakingly accurate picture of postwar refugee life. The "pale green farmworker triangles sewn chest-high on each blouse bobbing, drifting, at a certain hour of the dusk, like candleflames in religious procession," for example, are symbolically scaled-down versions of the farmer's traditional smock and were worn as defining badges by certain pro-Nazi elements among the Bavarian peasantry; and the fragment of dialogue dealing with the postwar potato famine—"stripped by the SS, Bruder, ja, every fucking potato field, and what for? Alcohol. Not to drink, no, alcohol for the rockets"— notes an important but generally disregarded way in which the V-2 continued to menace humanity long after the war was over.[28] As they multiply, such details provide so much intensity and depth that the effect, again, is of "a progressive *knotting into*—"(p. 3). There is no bottom to this description of migrating people, their costumes, their habits, their salvaged possessions, and their techniques for survival. And so this catalogue, like so many others in the novel, trails off in ellipses, suggesting at once the inexhaustible quality of even a clearly demarcated segment of lived experience and the sense in which this move of the dispossessed continues into the present, one aspect of the universal preterite condition.

Such catalogues are synecdoche with a vengeance. They parody the historical novelist's strategy of providing documentable "slices of life" from his period to increase the effect of verisimilitude. In Pynchon's hands historical details proliferate with such apparent abandon that they take over the text at several points, subverting conventional realism rather than supporting it by disrupting chronological sequence. The studious avoidance of anachronism does not function as a limit; it seems to justify the inclusion of every detail that might qualify as "period," so that the novel wallows in its setting, feeling out the particular sensuousness of each narrated incident.

In addition, *Gravity's Rainbow* appears obsessed with documentation and parades out-of-the-way information as if it were dedicated to providing material for source study. For example, Slothrop's investigations into his connections with Lazslo Jamf branch out in a number of directions, until the novel comes to incorporate most of the available information linking Shell Oil, Dupont, and General Electric to I.G.

Farben's wartime operation. A great deal of this information is of dubious relevance, however. When the narrator turns to the unsuccessful British attempts to build a rocket, he seems motivated only by the desire not to leave anything out, as if the history of V-2 development necessarily included everything having to do with rocketry: "A team ramrodded by one Isaac Lubbock set up a static-test facility at Langhurst near Horsham, and began to experiment with liquid oxygen and aviation fuel, running their first successful test in August of '42. Engineer Lubbock was a double first at Cambridge and the Father of British Liquid Oxygen Research . . ." (p. 240). On the other hand, the text occasionally provides *only* a reference, mocking the futility of trying to exhaust the "combinations 'n' permutations" of data: "(Check out Ishmael Reed. He knows more about it than you'll ever find here)" (p. 588).[29] At other times documentation blossoms into fantasy heavily tinged with paranoia:

> (later witnesses have suggested that Clerk Maxwell intended his Demon not so much as a convenience in discussing a thermodynamic idea as a parable about the *actual existence* of personnel like Liebig...we may gain an indication of how far the repression had grown by that time, in the degree to which Clerk Maxwell felt obliged to code his warnings...indeed some theorists, usually the ones who find sinister meaning behind even *Mrs.* Clerk Maxwell's notorious "It is time to go home, James, you are beginning to enjoy yourself," have made the extreme suggestion that the Field Equations themselves contain an ominous forewarning....) (P. 411; Pynchon's ellipses)

The "later witnesses" and "some theorists" of this passage gain credibility by association with the indubitably real James Clerk Maxwell, and through such vaguely defined "authorities" (standard props for the historian venturing into speculation) Pynchon can draw out occult implications in a parody of academic research. Further "experts" are pure invention, but Pynchon uses them in the same way he uses his verifiable sources; they provide a purportedly authoritative standard for evaluating information. Thus the "world-renowned analyst Mickey Wuxtry-Wuxtry" "opines" that Slothrop "might be in love, in sexual love, with his, and his race's, death" (p. 738), a statement that sounds portentous out of context but that gets exactly as much emphasis as the opinion of Natasha Raum, who writes in one of Pynchon's parodically "scholarly" journals, *Proceedings of the International Society of Confessors to an Enthusiasm for Albatross Nosology*, that fragments of Slothrop resemble "feathers . . . redundant or regenerable organs, 'which we would be tempted to classify under the "Hydra-Phänomen" were it not for the complete absence of hostility . . .'" (p. 712). Such "authorities" multiply perspectives rather than providing a single authoritative viewpoint. By incorporating both real and imagined outside testimony into the novel, Pynchon emphasizes the sheer impossibility of holding everything together.

The ellipses sprinkled intrusively through the text constitute a further indication of Pynchon's commitment to incompleteness in this novel (ellipses are not a stylistic feature of either *V.* or *The Crying of Lot 49*). Not only catalogues, but dialogues, narrative comments, and even whole sections trail off in strings of dots that suggest such passages could just as well go on. Sometimes the ellipses signal repetition, as in the brilliant section in chapter one that begins and ends with a movie camera following Katje as she moves through Osbie Feel's cottage (pp. 92–113). The framing device of the camera naturalizes the implication of infinite repetition by suggesting that the incident is one strip of film spliced end to end, playing over and over, a suggestion that is reinforced later when Katje discovers the film and screens it.[30] More often, however, the ellipses imply that an action, description, or train of thought simply goes on, further than the narrative can or will follow. In this way the novel presents itself as a collection of intricately interrelated but open-ended sections.[31] Even the ominous universality of the last sentence, "Now everybody—" does not guarantee closure. "There is time," even with annihilation delta-t away; there is always time as long as experience, parodying the abstract divisions of the infinitesimal calculus, continues to proliferate in unimagined directions. Instead of a concluding period, the novel offers an aposiopesis, explicitly inviting the reader to continue.

Even the length of *Gravity's Rainbow* (it is two-thirds again as long as *V.* and over five times as long as *Lot 49*) appears to derive from the ultimately futile project of trying to exhaust a historical period, and in this way to discover the antecedents of a present-day situation. By a principle dear to both the "cause-and-effect men" of the novel's world and writers of traditional narrative, the past is the cause of the present. Kermode has observed that the linear narrative has "a fixation on the eidetic imagery of beginning, middle, and end, potency and cause," because choices made early in the action necessarily limit the range of subsequent options.[32] Pynchon is able to circumvent this restriction and thus to leave the present open to surprises by undermining the stability of that apparently rigid entity, the past. If this past is going to necessitate even certain incidents in the present, there should be some agreement on just what it is—on what, exactly, has happened and on what events mean. Because of the fragmented narrative line and the shifting perspectives in *Gravity's Rainbow*, there is no general agreement on either of these points, although there are enclaves of agreement. As Pirate Prentice tells Roger Mexico, "We don't have to worry about questions of real or unreal. . . . It's the *system* that matters. How the data arrange themselves inside it. Some are consistent, others fall apart" (p. 638). The novel offers no standard of ultimate reality or unreality. It remains plural, open to any number of mutually contradictory, self-consistent, and non-exhaustive readings. By this token Pynchon suggests that history itself remains open and that no definitive interpretation can pinpoint the exact "place" of an event in the overall scheme of things. Even the rocket, which is the paradigm of an inflexible, spatialized view of history perceived *sub specie aeternitatis*, turns out to be open to multiple heretical readings.

> But the Rocket has to be many things, it must answer to a number of different shapes in the dreams of whose who touch it—in combat, in tunnel, on paper—it must survive heresies shining, unconfoundable...and heretics there will be: Gnostics who have been taken in a rush of wind and fire to chambers of the Rocket-throne ...Kabbalists who study the Rocket as Torah, letter by letter— rivets, burner cup and brass rose, its text is theirs to permute and combine into new revelations, always unfolding...Manicheans who see two Rockets, good and evil, who speak together in the sacred idiolalia of the Primal Twins (some say their names are Enzian and Blicero) of a good Rocket to take us to the stars, an evil Rocket for the World's suicide, the two perpetually in struggle. (P. 727; Pynchon's ellipses)

Despite the subsequent threat—"these heretics will be sought and the dominion of silence will enlarge as each one goes down...they will *all* be sought out"—there is no way to guarantee an orthodox reading of even technologically-conditioned history. Near the conclusion the V-2 becomes the central symbol of "any System which cannot tolerate heresy: a system which, by its nature, must sooner or later fall" (p. 747).[33]

A heresy is an unorthodox interpretation. It arises when a reader approaches a Text—a term usually capitalized in *Gravity's Rainbow* to indicate its enlarged extension: the rocket, the world, and the novel itself are all Texts—with assumptions and needs differing from the assumptions and needs that are officially defined. In other words, heresies stem from differences in perspective, and multiple perspectives breed multiple heresies. *Gravity's Rainbow* is made up of an enormous number of perspectives on something that gains a misleading solidity by being called "history," and these perspectives jostle for supremacy; each in its own way claims official sanction. By using Murphy's law to undermine all claims to ultimate authority, Pynchon provides the theoretical underpinning for a vision of history as a layering of heresies, without the possibility of an orthodoxy that can reconcile them, select among them, or rule them out. History in these terms is not a single set of relationships; it is a moiré of paranoias (p. 395), shifting emphasis endlessly as the point of view changes, a complex of communally defined We-systems and paranoiacally conceived They-systems. Any reader of the novel who undertakes the job of sorting out all these versions in the hope of arriving at a culminating insight must eventually recognize that any such insight would be disastrous. The joke is that such an insight is also impossible. Yet this does not reduce the multiple coherence systems of the book to incoherence. The ongoing project is one of making meanings, in the company of a vast panorama of characters engaged in the same activity. What emerges from this project is a recognition of community, and if "community" is a clichéd term, Pynchon's vision of it is rather startling because such a community does not depend on allegiance to any theoretical construction of reality. It depends instead on shared limitations and fears, the same limitations and fears that give rise to multiple readings of history.

Because he is apparently omniscient, the narrator of *Gravity's Rainbow* licenses both the proliferating points of view in the novel and the comprehensive sympathy that makes plurality compatible with community. By using the present tense, this narrator in effect occupies the action and insists that he is not in the traditionally godlike position of looking back on it. Appearing to speak from the action, he frequently addresses the reader, more like an on-the-spot reporter than a historian except that he has access to both the conscious and the unconscious psychic processes of the characters. If he is by these criteria an omniscient narrator, his omniscience does not make him a transcendent narrator. He remains, like the characters, inside history, and thus he appears to know everything except what will happen.[34]

This narrator differs from the traditional novel's godlike

intermediary in another important respect. He is even less evidently a ''he'' than most narrators, not only because he has no determinate gender but because he is not even unequivocally unitary. (He remains misleadingly singular and male in this discussion only because I have no terminology for dealing easily with such a presence.) If the adjective ''omniscient'' is to be applied to him, it needs to be untangled from its usual Judeo-Christian associations, for this speaker is a Proteus who can change tone and attitude so completely that his utterances appear to emanate from separate personae. He is capable of lofty, if slightly skewed, meditations on the significance of the action he is relating, as in this lament for Slothrop's failed epiphany:

> There is no good reason to hope for any turn, any surprise *I-see-it*, not from Slothrop. Here he is, scaling the walls of an honest ceremonial plexus, set down on a good enough vision of what's shadowless noon and what isn't. But oh, Egg the flying Rocket hatched from, navel of the 50-meter radio sky, all proper ghosts of place—forgive him his numbness, his glozing neutrality. Forgive the fist that doesn't tighten in his chest, the heart that can't stiffen in any greeting....Forgive him as you forgave Tchitcherine at the Kirghiz Light....Better days are coming. (Pp. 509–10, Pynchon's ellipses)

On the other hand, he is equally liable to lapse into exaggerated colloquialism, especially in passages that invoke the drug experience as a naturalizing convention.[35] The following passage deals with the same general subject as the previous one, epiphanic revelation, but here revelation emerges as a far less ultimate issue because the frenzied delivery suggests the speaker might with equal probability be insane, hallucinating, or engaged in a put-on:

> Well, it's a matter of continuity. Most people's lives have ups and downs that are relatively gradual, a sinuous curve with first derivatives at every point. They're the ones who never get struck by lightning. No real idea of cataclysm at all. But the ones who do get hit experience a singular point, a discontinuity in the curve of

life—do you know what the time rate of change *is* at a cusp? *Infinity*, that's what! A-and right across the point, it's *minus* infinity! How's *that* for sudden change, eh? Infinite miles per hour changing to the same speed *in reverse*, all in the gnat's-ass or red cunt hair of the Δt across the point. That's getting hit by lightning, folks. (P. 664)

Such radical shifts in diction, tone, and perspective make it very difficult to maintain that the same narrator presides over the action from one moment to the next. If the narrator is omniscient, he is also irreconcilably plural, a cacophony of voices, each knowing a different version of everything.

One factor that individualizes the narrator in his successive manifestations is something that Hugh Kenner, discussing Joyce, has identified as the Uncle Charles Principle. According to this principle, the narrative voice becomes warped by proximity to a character so that it picks up distinctive habits of thought and verbal tics.[36] In *Gravity's Rainbow* the Uncle Charles Principle contributes to the plurality of narrative voices. For example, passages featuring Slothrop become infiltrated by Slothropian mannerisms: "The ape reaches up taps Slothrop on the ass, hands him what he's been carrying yaahhgghh it's a round black iron anarchist's *bomb*'s what it is, with *lit fuse* too...." (p. 689). The description of "Pfc. Eddie Pensiero, a replacement here in the 89th Division, also an amphetamine enthusiast," picks up Eddie's speed-freak intensity: "But the gift isn't limited just to Eddie's *own* shivers, oh no, they're *other* peoples' shivers, too! Yeah they come in one by one, they come all together in groups . . . " (p. 641). And the report on the Argentine Felipe's Teilhardian thesis about the secret life of rocks is heavily influenced by Felipe's hepcat language: "But Felipe has come to see, as those who are not Sentient Rocksters seldom do, that history as it's been laid on the world is only a fraction, an outward-and-visible fraction" (p. 612). Characters speak through the narrator, or the narrator moves in to embrace and envelop individual characters.

The effect is of multiple "inside" perspectives with no "outside" standard against which to measure them.

The fact that the narrator refuses to stand aloof from the characters has implications for the value systems of *Gravity's Rainbow*. The novel deals with some of the most horrifying prospects of contemporary life: the rise of megalithic international corporations, the corresponding dehumanization of twentieth-century society, the immanent purposes of technology, the threat of global annihilation. But though the text insists on a polarized vision with indelible lines drawn between Us and Them, it does not condemn any of its characters. The narrator treats even the most villainous figures with such compassion that it becomes impossible to regard the novel's world as populated by villains and heroes. A villain can stay a villain only if he is regarded from a rigorously "objective" standpoint, and this narrator eschews objectivity to such a degree that the reader is forced to understand and even sympathize with conventionally repellent types like Pointsman and Blicero. In a way, such sympathy is more shocking that pronounced antipathy because it insists that there is no real They in the final analysis: only Us.

For this reason there is no way to draw a line between redeemed and unredeemed characters. The issue of redemption implicitly invokes a transcendent moral arbiter who divides humanity into Elect and Preterite. Although certain characters attempt to transcend the world of the novel, transcendence is impossible; the great irony is that everyone is Preterite, and They are only a perverted ideal. It is in the pathetic attempt to become Them that characters erect totalitarian "structures favoring death"—only to find themselves trapped within these structures. And it is the pathos of this situation that the narrator is able to communicate because he speaks from inside the action and even from inside characters.

Pointsman, for instance, would seem to be a clear example of a bad guy within the overall context. Not only has he pledged himself to antihuman ideals (rather like Fritz Lang's mad scientist Dr. Mabuse, who lurks as a possible paradigm behind all the scientifically-minded characters), but his attempts to explain Slothrop turn Slothrop into a pariah and a scapegoat for the devastations of the V-2. Furthermore, Pointsman's motives are unpleasantly tinged with perverse sexuality. Early in the book the narrator introduces his fixation on experiments with human subjects:

> How Pointsman lusts after them, pretty children. Those drab undershorts of his are full to bursting with need humorlessly, worldly to use their innocence, to write on them new words of himself, his own brown Realpolitik dreams, some psychic prostate ever in aching love promised, ah hinted but till now... (P. 50)

"—ugh, creepy, creepy," is Jessica's reaction—not to Pointsman's fixation, as it happens, but to Slothrop's. It is a reaction the reader is rarely allowed, at least not in the process of reading. For the narrator does not view Pointsman from a distance in order to incorporate him into an overall context. In Pointsman's case, as in Slothrop's, the narrator probes further into the character, establishing an intimacy so intense that the outsider's perspective becomes specious. After two paragraphs developing Pointsman's illicit desire to kidnap a child for use as an experimental subject—a child who at first is presented as a typical war orphan in a typical Pavlovian pick-up situation—the referent changes. The narrator, who has been talking about Pointsman, suddenly begins talking *to* "you." The details become acutely particular and concrete. The purportedly general and representative situation takes on painful immediacy.

> You have waited in these places into the early mornings, synced in to the on-whitening of the interior, you know the Arrivals schedule by heart, by hollow heart. And where these children have run away from, and that, in this city, there is no one to meet them. You impress them with your gentleness. You've never quite decided if they can see through to your vacuum. They won't yet look in your eyes, their slender legs are never still, knitted stockings droop (all elastic has gone to war), but charm-

ingly: little heels kick restless against the canvas bags, the fraying valises under the wood bench. Speakers in the ceiling report departures and arrivals in English, then in the other, exile languages. Tonight's child has had a long trip here, hasn't slept. Her eyes are red, her frock wrinkled. Her coat has been a pillow. You feel her exhaustion, feel the impossible vastness of all the sleeping countryside at her back, and for the moment you really are selfless, sexless...considering only how to shelter her, you are the Traveler's Aid. (Pp. 50–51; Pynchon's ellipsis)

This passage is extraordinarily powerful because it identifies completely with the situation, with its intrinsic horror and also with its tenderness. The carefully delineated frame for this moment dissolves, and the effect is to bring the reader into the picture, transforming his implicit voyeurism into imaginative participation. With the dissolution of this boundary, Pynchon can provoke a recognition of how tenuous the line is separating concern from exploitation, cherishing from destroying. If Pointsman is caught between apparently conflicting desires that are terrifying precisely because they do not conflict, the thoroughly equivocal "you" of this passage insists that the reader understands, knows how it feels. At this moment of urgency, external standards of judgment are irrelevant. Then the tension relaxes; the description fades into another string of ellipses, and the narrator returns to the framing story with the humorously brutal transition, "Yet for all his agonizing all Pointsman will score, presently, is an octopus" (p. 51). But this passage (like several subsequent passages renewing the intimacy with Pointsman) undermines the comfortable assumption that the Pavlovian is an alien, an "unredeemable" character who can be dismissed from concern because his obsessions are simply inexplicable from a sanctioned perspective.

Such moments are frequent in the novel, although not all of them are as intense or as unsettling. The narrator tends to modulate into direct address whenever a character says or does something that might alienate the reader and provoke an unsympathetically pejorative judgment, as when Jessica "has gone into her Fay Wray number," a move that unnerves her anxious lover, the thoroughly likeable Roger Mexico, and seems on the face of things an unwarranted affectation. But here the narrator intervenes with a helpful gloss: "This is a kind of protective paralysis, akin to your own response when the moray eel jumps you from the ceiling" (p. 275). Although the comparison, of course, does not appeal to common experience (which is why it is funny), it does compel imaginative assent. Jessica's action becomes intuitively intelligible and thus sympathetic.

One index of the narrator's protean capacity to enter into the motives and desires of the characters is the way that Blicero, the Nazi, sadist, sexual pervert, nihilist, and murderer, emerges as disconcertingly comprehensible and almost tragic. Blicero kills his paramour and symbolic son, Gottfried (whose name, "the peace of God," is heavily ironic), out of intense loathing for the natural world. By invoking an alluring synthesis of Greek and Hebrew mythology, German idealism, and Kabbalized technology, the narrator is able to communicate both this loathing and the extent to which it permeates Western civilization:

> "Want the Change," Rilke said, "O be inspired by the Flame!" To laurel, to nightingale, to wind...*wanting* it, to be taken, to embrace, to fall toward the flame growing to fill all the senses and...not to love because it was no longer possible to act...but to be helplessly in a condition of love.... (p. 97; Pynchon's ellipses)[37]

By an archetypal and eerily seductive displacement, Blicero translates Rilkean self-surrender to filicide, so that in the closing sections he plays Abraham to Gottfried's Isaac (pp. 749–50), acting out a familiar paradigm of denying human ties in obedience to a seemingly irrational higher will. By sacrificing his "son" to the rocket, Blicero offers a grisly parody of acceptance. This "acceptance" is really a repudiation of his own involvement in the natural cycle, "this cycle of infection and death'' (p. 724), and in a moment of dreadful sincerity he tells Gottfried that his horror of his own mortality prompts him to make a burnt offering of the younger man:

> oh Gottfried of course yes you are beautiful to me but I'm dying... I want to get through it as honestly as I can, and your immortality rips at my heart—can't you see why I might want to destroy that, oh that *stupid clarity* in your eyes...when I see you in morning and evening ranks, so open, so ready to take my sickness in and shelter it, shelter it inside your own little ignorant love.... (P. 723, Pynchon's ellipses)

In this moment, when Blicero reveals that his infatuation with the rocket's version of the providential trajectory stems from jealousy and self-loathing, he is disturbingly sympathetic. It is not only his honesty that is unsettling; it is also the implication that allegiance to any of the totalizing "structures favoring death" arises from such quintessentially human motives.

In paying allegiance to the rocket's cosmology, Blicero attempts to transcend both mortality and concern—the two are inseparable in *Gravity's Rainbow*. His example is representative of the way in which totalizing structures minimize relations of caring between individuals. Pökler's immersion in the intricacies of rocket design "allowed him to put as much labyrinth as required between himself and the inconveniences of caring" (p. 428); and this description reflects the attitude of scientists like Peenemünde chief Walter Dornberger, who wrote a whole book, *V-2*, on his experiences with the rocket development program without once mentioning the fact, forced painfully on Pökler, that the assembly plant at Nordhausen was staffed by slave laborers from the concentration camp Dora; or like Wernher von Braun, who in his *History of Rocketry and Space Travel* seems concerned only with the business of sending rockets up, not with where they came down. Similarly, Pointsman and Roger Mexico are so engrossed in the respective merits of causality and statistical probability as ways of explaining why V-2 strikes follow

Slothrop's apparent pattern of conquests that it is Jessica who has to ask the obvious question, "what about the girls?" (p. 87). Unifying theories, regardless of their capacity to reconcile quantitative data, provide little room for compassion.

By contrast, the narrative voice is all-embracing by virtue of the fact that it embraces each character and concern separately. By taking a succession of points of view and accepting the limitations intrinsic to each, the narrator defers closure, and with each deferral emphasizes the futility of trying to image experience as a coherent state of affairs. Such a totalized theoretical "state" has as its political corollary the totalitarian state, and in *Gravity's Rainbow* all such "states" are both artificial and arbitrary. Throughout the novel, systems, structures, overarching frameworks, and plots alternately promise solace and despair, but all of them help falsify the fact of mortality and all of them obscure the bonds between individual human beings. "The basic problem," the dope salesman Wimpe tells Tchitcherine, "has always been getting other people to die for you. What's worth enough for a man to give up his life? That's where religion had the edge, for centuries. Religion was always about death" (p. 701). Religions change—Wimpe is discussing Marxism—but their purpose remains to subsume human concerns to the bogus will of a higher principle. Even as a Soviet spy, however, Tchitcherine has served something different, "a mortal State that will persist no longer than the individuals in it" (p. 338). The emergent Counterforce picks up this idea and expands its implications. "The dearest nation of all is one that will survive no longer than you and I, a common movement at the mercy of death and time: the ad hoc adventure" (p. 706).

Implicit in this resolution drawn up by a sort of Preterite Maquis of the Zone's inhabitants is the idea that the only unity worth bothering about is the transient community of people who have come together around the acknowledgement of their common frailty. When Slothrop meets Geli Tripping the narrator observes, "Slothrop, though he doesn't know it yet, is as properly constituted a state as any other in the Zone these days. Not paranoia. Just how it is. Temporary alliances, knit and undone" (p. 291). Such temporary alliances reflect the temporary nature of human life; they are based on personal relations—friendship, loyalty, love—not on eternal links in a cosmic plan. An earlier namesake of Tchitcherine believed in "a State that would outlive them all, where someone would come to sit in his seat at the table just as he had slipped into Trotsky's" (p. 338); and when Slothrop thinks about leaving Bianca, the narrator asks insidiously, "Why bring her back? Why try? It's only the difference between the real boxtop and the one you draw for Them" (p. 472). The rationale is similar to the one that sent Pökler a daughter who was an assembly built up of successive summer "frames." But this notion of fixed roles with interchangeable players presumes that history is an eternal drama already written.

The alternative is a shifting network of relations that are continually being created and destroyed. Temporary alliances make connections—make meanings, in fact. In *Gravity's Rainbow* contingent communities spontaneously generate new patterns of relation, new myths, and especially new language out of the awareness that a primal unity is forever out of reach. Communities arise among people who perceive themselves as fallen: victimized, frail, fallible, and mortal. Language is similarly fallen, removed from a postulated condition in which words were indivisible from the things they stood for. But in its endless proliferation as it flies from the center, language becomes the flowering of community. In taking words apart and putting them together in new combinations, groups bent on making sense effectively make different realities, although in accordance with Murphy's law such realities emerge in startling and unexpected forms. The eccentric propagandists who achieve a precarious solidarity at "the White Visitation" dream up a "Schwarzkommando" to scare the Germans only to find that the Schwarzkommando exist, as if they had been willed into being to provide this fringe of the bureaucracy with a fresh and absorbing Black Problem and a new lexicon of technical terms to investigate: "Schwarzphänomenon," Schwarzgerät," and Slothrop's dream-coinages "Black-woman," "Blackrocket," "Blackdream" (p. 391). The Schwarzkommando themselves are among the most prolific coiners. Even the attempts of their splinter group, the Empty Ones, to evolve a theoretical justification for racial suicide gives rise to neologisms like "Otukungurua. Yes, old Africa hands, it *ought* to be 'Omakungurua,' but they are always careful—perhaps it's less healthy than care—to point out that *oma-* applies only to the living and human. *Otu-* is for the inanimate and the rising, and this is how they imagine them-selves" (pp. 316–17). Paradoxically, these new Blackwords act as the reconciling process for the emerging society, gener-ating an eclectic mythology that is part tradition and part tech-nology, a system of worship, and a Text based on the rocket that inevitably engenders multiple heresies rendering the Text incomplete and leaving the Herero destiny open to new gener-ations of Kabbalists.

The Hereros, like the Puritans, cling to names as relics of the original Word, the revelation that has passed them over. Like the original inhabitants of Eden they accord the act of naming metaphysical significance, groping after an original copresence of words and things. If primal unity eludes them, the nostalgia for such unity makes them sensitive to the ways words set up Kute Korrespondences and point to unimagined connections:

North is death's region. There may be no gods, but there is a pattern: names by themselves may have no magic, but the *act* of naming, the physical utterance, obeys the pattern. Nordhausen means dwellings in the north. The Rocket had to be produced out of a place called Nordhausen. The town adjoining was named Bleicheröde as a validation, a bit of redundancy so that the message would not be lost. The history of the old Hereros is one of lost messages. (P. 322)

This awareness of resemblances, fostered by an acute sense of having always missed the messages, gives the Hereros privileged insight into the linguistic slippages that multiply significance in *Gravity's Rainbow*. Nordhausen was the actual location of the V-2 Mittelwerke; it also points to the Herero region of death. The propriety of this name is reinforced by the proximity of Nordhausen to Bleicheröde, where, not incidentally, the Peenemünde scientists gave themselves up to the Allies.[38] "Bleicheröde" sounds like "Blicero," which in turn suggests "blicker," from the Old German "to bleach," and links the word to the Herero color of death, white, the color encoded in Blicero's other name, Weissmann, and the color of the alien culture that threatens to kill the black emigrants. In presenting a cast of characters who are particularly sensitive to the latent connotations of names and the ways in which these connotations set up new chains of association, Pynchon can provoke wonder at the peculiar propriety of names that people have actually bestowed. There is some irony in the fact that the German film capital was called Neubabelsberg, for instance, and more in the fact that the Enzian, the mountain gentian immortalized by Rilke, was also a V-weapon, a surface-to-air missile.[39] The Hereros believe that the act of naming obeys a pattern, but in *Gravity's Rainbow* the act of naming sets up patterns that multiply implications without ever resolving into a single, culminating message.

Technical terminology also triggers latent correspondences that reach out in all directions, setting up new networks of associations. As the narrator points out, the SS symbol for the double integral also signifies Hitler's secret police, the shape of the tunnels in the Mittelwerke, the rune that stands for the yew tree, itself a symbol of death, and the shape of lovers curled asleep (pp. 301–2). The associations are evocative; they do not integrate to a clear revelation. Indeed, the mathematical symbol appears to prompt meanings to burgeon, like that "determinist . . . piece of hardware" the V-2, which in the discussion of Murphy's law begins "spontaneously generating items like the 'S-Gerät' Slothrop thinks he's chasing like a grail" (p. 275). New languages signal fecundity in *Gravity's Rainbow*. Enzian was born from a transient union between a Russian sailor and a Herero woman, and the couple out of necessity invented "the beginnings of a new tongue, a pidgin which they were perhaps the only two speakers of in the world" (p. 351). "Raketemensch!" screams Saüre Bummer, and the appellation spawns a full-fledged, if inept, superhero. "Names by themselves may be empty," comments the narrator, "but the *act of naming...*" (p. 366).

The act of naming is the common human act in this novel. It stems from a perception of inadequacy: both people and language are severely limited. Humanity has fallen into time and mortality; words have fallen from the original Word. People make meanings in the absence of certainty. But the project of making meanings has its own continuity, although the meanings change. It is an open-ended project and a messy one, covering pristine surfaces with proliferating language, "the Word made printer's ink" (p. 571), another manifestation of the unsettling blackness that characters committed to totalizing structures would rather erase. Blicero's murder of Gottfried is such an erasure, for Gottfried is sacrificed on the altar of the rocket, the principle of totalization and thus of hierarchy and subordination. The rocket dictates that the sweep of history arches over trivial human lives. As he careens toward death, Gottfried witnesses the whiting-out of his own personal experience as he is assimilated to the providential trajectory.

> ...what is this death but a whitening, a carrying of whiteness to ultrawhite, what is it but bleaches, detergents, oxidizers, abrasives—Streckefuss he's been today to the boy's tormented muscles, but more appropriately is he Blicker, Bleicheröde, Bleacher, Blicero, extending, rarefying the Caucasian pallor to an abolition of pigment, of melanin, of spectrum, of separateness from shade to shade, it is *so white that* CATCH the dog was a red setter, the last dog's head, the kind dog come to see him off *can't remember what red meant*, the pigeon he chased was slate blue, but they're both white now beside the canal that night the smell of trees *oh I didn't want to lose that night* CATCH. . . . (P. 759)

In this passage all the associations of whiteness come together to mock the reader's desire to white out the text by sacrificing its sprawl of language to the incandescence of a revelatory conclusion. If he accepts such a conclusion, the reader cannot stand outside it. "Now everybody—" denies anyone's Election and at the same time denies the abstract satisfaction of conventional closure.

Gravity's Rainbow gets most of its energy from denying the validity of this kind of abstraction. To abstract is to generalize, but it is also, and more insidiously, to stand apart from, and it is standing apart that becomes the lie in this novel. In a sense Pynchon flirts with the impossible: he tries to confront his readers with their own mortality, vulnerability, and preterition. This last term, "preterition," is the most overtly technical; in Puritan theology it is also the most nearly empty, designating the negative category of those who are not chosen. In increasing the extension of this word until it covers everyone, Pynchon also multiplies its connotations until the novel becomes the attentive, compassionate exploration of what it means to belong to that transient community, the mortal state. From the vantage of Election, preterition is exclusion from the providential plan. But because the Preterite are not included in the plan, they are not defined from outside, and this condition allows them possibility. If the Preterite are the waste of the system, they are also like the "preterite dung" of Rathenau's visionary earth, infinitely diverse and pregnant with potential. In a novel that wallows in excremental imagery, it is worth noting that Pynchon grants shit a great deal of significance— and a great deal of variety. The Hereros, like the proverbial Eskimos who have nineteen words for nineteen different kinds of snow, make linguistic discriminations between different kinds of shit (p. 325). They have more intimacy with the subject, a fact that follows from their acute awareness of their own status as human detritus. From an outside standpoint, the standpoint of a hypothesized Them, all of humanity is shit. People in abstraction can be grouped as an undifferentiated mass of waste, and by a political euphemism they become the

People. *Gravity's Rainbow* denies its readers the privilege of standing outside the People, dealing with them and dismissing them. The outside perspective is not a human perspective.[40]

The book contains a sort of manifesto to this effect, a segment of an ongoing chronicle that mysteriously "passes for" Katje and Prentice in an equally mysterious section taking place in a city that may be hell but that is also the place where betrayed and betrayer come together to acknowledge their mutual dependence.

There passes for Pirate and Katje a brief segment of a much longer chronicle, the anonymous *How I Came to Love the People*. "Her name was Brenda, her face was the bird under the projecting grin of the car in the rain that morning, she knelt and performed fellatio on me, and I ejaculated on her breasts. Her name was Lily, she was 67 last August, she reads off the labels of beer bottles to herself out loud, we coupled in the standard English position, and she patted me on the back and whispered 'Good friend.' His name was Frank, his hair curled away from his face, his eyes were rather sharp but pleasant, he stole from American Army depots, he bum-fucked me and when he came inside me, so did I. Her name was Frangibella, she was black, her face was broken out, she wanted money for dope, her openness was a viper writhing in my heart, I performed cunnilingus upon her. His name was Allan, his buttocks were tanned, I said, where did you find the sun, he answered, the sun is just around the corner, I held him over the pillow and buggered him and he cried with love till I, my piston pungently greased, exploded at last. Her name was Nancy, she was six, we went behind a wall near a crater full of ruins, she rubbed and rubbed against me, her milky little thighs reaching in and out of my own, her eyes were closed, her fair little nostrils moved upward, backward forever, the slope of debris rushed down, steeply, just beside us, we teetered at the edge, on and on, exquisitely. Her name was—" well, all these and many more pass for our young couple here, enough to make them understand that horny Anonymous's intentions are nothing less than a megalomaniac master plan of sexual love with every individual one of the People in the *World*—and that when every one, somewhat miraculously, is accounted for at last, *that* will be a rough definition of "loving the People." (P. 547)

The project obviously can never be completed: "the People" expands geometrically as horny Anonymous proceeds one-on-one. "How I Came to Love the People" is another system that refuses to close because its author shuns the falsifications of totality. In its way this piece is a microcosm of the whole book, a segment of an unrealizable project. In its intimacy, which is also the intimacy of pornography, it betrays the bogus abstraction of its title, approaching a "rough definition" of the whole asymptotically without ever being able to close.

Gravity's Rainbow is another mammoth project of loving the people, loving even their preterition in its scatalogical profusion, avoiding a univocal standard of judgment, avoiding hierarchy, and demanding a miraculous sympathy for every aspect of the mortal state. For all its preoccupation with ideas, the novel emphasizes relations of concern over totalizing structures. It insists that explanatory systems are always *somebody's* explanatory systems by attributing them to characters or to the narrator in one of his highly personalized manifestations. Ideas come from people; they are never autonomous. For this reason *Gravity's Rainbow* is not a novel in which, as Scott Simmon claimed, things are more important than people and ideas are more important than things, [41] although it exploits the familiarity and attraction of this thesis by inviting readers to construct explanatory structures that imprison them. It is instead a novel that affirms the nonsystematic, nontotalizing connections of a community based on making meanings. To understand the infinitely various ways in which human beings deal with their common fear by exfoliating networks of significance and language is to love the People—and this is an inexhaustible project by definition. It is the project that *Gravity's Rainbow* undertakes, with humor, compassion, and a conspicuous lack of sentimentality.

Gravity's Rainbow is the first novel in which Pynchon refuses to subsume his absurd, exaggerated, perverse, and sometimes destructive characters to their ideas. To understand history is to understand that history can have no definitive shape; it is also to understand where paranoid notions of a preformed destiny come from. In *V.* the elderly explorer Hugh Godolphin saw in Vheissu a "dream of annihilation"; and *Gravity's Rainbow* deals with the same dream but affirms that it is a human dream, originating with human beings who prefer to look forward to global catastrophe rather than to acknowledge their own mortality. The rocket is a "dream of flight" from human limitations, even if it promises racial extinction. But these same limitations suggest that even a race sold on suicide may not accomplish its goal. The only inevitability is that something will go wrong, something will surprise us.

"I don't think any of us has recognized just how radical Pynchon is," Raymond Olderman wrote in a recent review.[42] The recognition is difficult because Pynchon offers deceptive "handles" on all his books, possible readings that gain persuasiveness by leading to unwelcome conclusions. In *Gravity's Rainbow* an interpretation guided by the rocket's trajectory counsels such complete despair that it appears inescapable, simply because it is so depressing. But this tendency to accept nihilism as tough-mindedness is what Pynchon satirizes in this novel. *Gravity's Rainbow* confronts its readers with the spectacle of a postreligious society committed to a vision of apocalypse, and duplicitously invites them to share this vision by trying to fit outrageous humor into a predestined tragic pattern. The comedy results from the fact that things do not fit. No conceivable providence can control the wealth and diversity of such secular history.

Notes

Introduction

1. *Poetics Today*, Vol. 1, nos. 1–2 (1979), pp. 86–110.

2. For a fuller exposition of this reading, see Frank Lentricchia, *The Gaiety of Language: An Essay on the Radical Poetics of W. B. Yeats and Wallace Stevens*, pp. 148–92.

3. I develop this argument in chapter 4, especially in the discussion of Murphy's Law's equivalence to Gödel's theorem. See also Werner Heisenberg's essay " 'Closed Theory' in Modern Science," in his collection of essays, *Across the Frontiers*.

4. William Paley, *Natural Theology: Selections*, pp. 3–12; Sir Isaac Newton, *Mathematical Principles of Natural Philosophy and System of the World*, p. 544.

Chapter One

1. *Gravity's Rainbow* (New York: Viking, 1973), pp. 703, 434, Pynchon's italics. Hereafter abbreviations cited in the text refer to the following editions: *GR, Gravity's Rainbow*; *Lot 49, The Crying of Lot 49* (New York: Bantam, 1967); *V.* (New York: Bantam, 1964).

2. Oedipa herself comes up with four possibilities (p. 128), but they resolve into this polarity.

3. Pynchon's parody of the Aristotelian plot is especially clear in *Gravity's Rainbow*, where rising action and falling action are graphed onto the trajectory of the V-2 rocket. I enlarge on this theme in chapter 4.

4. Pynchon borrows this complex of ideas from the *The Education of Henry Adams*. Although Adams's influence is especially evident in *V.*, the idea of a point of historical discontinuity is central to all three novels. Pynchon seems to view Adams as a key spokesman for modernism. And of course Adams is fascinated by the order/chaos dilemma and, in the *Education*, at least, is unable to evade it.

5. For a detailed exposition of this thesis, see Frank Kermode's classic study *The Sense of an Ending: Studies in the Theory of Fiction*.

6. Michael Holquist and Walter Reed observe that realism is an essential property of novels, regardless of their cultural context or degree of formal experimentation. The reason, they argue, is that the novel is generally committed to the recognition that the denotative system of a culture is inadequate to its connotative system. "This recognition of the exhaustibility of all systems, or their leaks, is what permits it to seem real in various cultures, no matter how diverse their ontologies, all of whose other texts presume a greater semiotic closure" ("Six Theses on the Novel—and Some Metaphors," p. 418.

7. This tendency has been especially pronounced in review articles, which of course prepare the way for more thorough studies. Two reviews of *Gravity's Rainbow* representative of this tendency to read "hermetically" are Josephine Hendin's laudatory "What Is Thomas Pynchon Telling Us?", p. 90, and Richard Locke's more dubious review in the *New York Times Book Review*, p. 14.

8. See especially William M. Plater, *The Grim Phoenix: Reconstructing Thomas Pynchon*. Robert Scholes offers a version of this theory as a defining condition of the genre he calls fabulation. See his *Fabulation and Metafiction*, pp. 1–20.

9. Such thinkers maintain that, on the contrary, human experience is necessarily "wall-to-wall discourse," to borrow Edward Said's description.

10. Alvin Greenberg, "The Underground Woman: An Excursion into the V-ness of Thomas Pynchon."

11. Louis Mackey aligns this "falling short" with the rhetorical figure *praeteritio* (better known in its Greek form, *paraleipsis*), "the figure of conspicuous omission. Omission by mention, or mention by omission," in his excellent essay, "Paranoia, Pynchon, and Preterition," p. 20. And in another fine essay, "The Mandala in *Gravity's Rainbow*," John M. Muste finds in the "O" at the center of the Herero mandala "the zero beyond which we may or may not go, the emptiness which all the characters try to fill, the 'progressive knotting into' which tries 'to bring events to Absolute Zero,' the silence, the empty Kirghiz plains; it is, in fine, 'the nothing that is.' "

12. *Summa Theologica*, part 1, question 13, article 5.

13. The modern, deterministic understanding of causality derives from Newton's formulation of the universal law of gravitation. I develop some of the implications of this association in chapter 4.

14. Introduction to Lincoln Barnett, *The Universe and Dr. Einstein*, p. 10.

15. In "Thomas Pynchon, Gödel's Theorem, the Rhetoric of Mathematics," an unpublished paper presented at the 1977 MLA session "The Meeting of Two Worlds: Literature and Science," Steven Weisenburger notes that "Mapping on to different coordinate systems" refers to the method by which Gödel's theorem established the impossibility of there ever being a complete mathematical-logical system. I deal with Gödel's theorem at some length in chapter 4.

16. *The Modes of Modern Writing: Metaphor, Metonymy, and the Typology of Modern Literature.*

17. As Brian McHale puts it, " 'mapping' is mimetically motivated." See his excellent article "Modernist Reading, Post-Modern Text: The Case of *Gravity's Rainbow*," p. 104. Another intelligent treatment of Pynchon's *thematic* commitments to language is Charles Russell's "Pynchon's Language: Signs. Systems, and Subversion," in Charles Clerc, ed., *Approaches to "Gravity's Rainbow."*

18. For an alternative view, see Thomas H. Schaub, *Pynchon: The Voice of Ambiguity*, especially pp. 3–20.

Chapter Two

1. See Fredric V. Bogel, "Fables of Knowing: Melodrama and Related Forms."

2. For other treatments of the order-chaos dichotomy, see especially Tony Tanner, "Caries and Cabals (Thomas Pynchon)," in his *City of Words: American Fiction, 1950–1970*, pp. 153–80, and chapter 3, " 'V.,' " of his more recent study, *Thomas Pynchon*, pp. 40–55; Robert E. Golden, "Mass Man and Modernism: Violence in Pynchon's *V.*"; David Richter, "The Failure of Completeness," in his *Fable's End*, pp. 101–35; Joseph Slade, "The Track of the Energy," in his *Thomas Pynchon*, pp. 48–124; W. T. Lhamon, Jr., "Pentecost, Promiscuity, and Pynchon's *V.*: From the Scaffold to the Impulsive"; Richard Patteson, "What Stencil Knew: Structure and Certitude in Pynchon's *V.*"; Scott Sanders, "Pynchon's Paranoid History"; Edward Mendelson's Introduction to *Pynchon: A Collection of Critical Essays*, pp. 1–15; Melvin New, "Profaned and Stenciled Texts: In Search of Pynchon's *V.*"

3. I am grateful to Richard Dunn for having suggested the last two examples.

4. Robert Musil, *The Man without Qualities*, 1:436.

5. Stencil is identified with the twentieth century throughout *V.* Born in 1901, he is "the century's child" (p. 42).

6. Ludwig Wittgenstein, *Philosophical Investigations*, 66 (p. 32^e). One of Wittgenstein's comments in this discussion might be a critique of Stencil's assumptions about narrative unity: "the strength of the thread does not reside in the fact that some one fibre runs through its whole length, but in the overlapping of many fibres" (67; p. 32e).

7. George Levine cites in addition *vécu*, "Sartre's term for 'lived experience,' " and Richard Leverenz's "*V.* is you," reinforcing the suggestion that Vheissu is as overdetermined as V. See his "Risking the Moment: Anarchy and Possibility in Pynchon's Fiction," in *Mindful Pleasures: Essays on Thomas Pynchon*, p. 136, n. 4.

8. In "The Dynamo and the Virgin," the chapter of the *Education* that bears most directly on *V.*, Adams writes, "Adams knew nothing about any

of [the forces acting on Western civilization], but as a mathematical problem of influence on human progress, though all were occult, all reacted on his mind, and he rather inclined to think the Virgin easiest to handle" (*The Education of Henry Adams*, p. 389). Stencil, of course, models himself on Adams, and the metaphor of historian-as-oyster used to describe him in chapter five also originates with the *Education*. In *V.* the metaphor is associated with Stencil's reconstructing activities: "Around each seed of a dossier, therefore, had developed a nacreous mass of inference, poetic license, forcible dislocation of personality into a past he didn't remember and had no right in save the right of imaginative anxiety or historical care, which is recognized by no one" (p. 51). Adams's analogous observation in his chapter 31, "The Grammar of Science," suggests that such activities reshape history to fit preexisting aesthetic norms: "As history unveiled itself in the new order, man's mind had behaved like a young pearl oyster, secreting its universe to suit its conditions until it had built up a shell of *nacre* that embodied all its notions of the perfect" (p. 458).

9. A version of one of the "past" chapters, "In which Stencil . . . " did appear as a short story in *Noble Savage* two years before the publication of *V.*

10. See his *The Modes of Modern Writing: Metaphor, Metonymy, and the Typology of Modern Literature.*

11. See Steven Weisenburger, "The End of History? Thomas Pynchon and the Uses of the Past."

12. Both Mondaugen and Weissmann are transposed into this context in *Gravity's Rainbow.* Furthermore, the horse Firelily, who figures prominently in Mondaugen's dream, is metamorphosed into one of the Third Reich's V-weapons, the surface-to-air missile Feuerlily. See Wernher von Braun and Frederick I. Ordway III, *A History of Rocketry and Space Travel*, p. 112.

13. Mafia is a parody of Ayn Rand, whose influence was at its peak in the early sixties when *V.* appeared.

14. James Ogilvy points out that decadence is also de-cadence, the refusal to return to the tonic and achieve unambiguous closure. See his *Many Dimensional Man: Decentralizing Self, Society, and the Sacred*, p. 176. By this token, if a decadence signals the Last Days, it also suggests that the whole concept of Last Days rests on an intuition of a nonexistent providential "plot." *V.* plays on the ambiguity.

Chapter Three

1. See, for instance, two influential reviews of *V.*, Jeremy Larner's "The New Schlemihl" and George Plimpton's "Mata Hari With a Clockwork Eye, Alligators in the Sewer."

2. Oedipa and the reader possess the same information. For this reason

Oedipa appears to be a more authoritative guide to interpretation than Stencil in *V.* or any of the major questing characters (Slothrop, Katje, Prentice, Mexico, Tchitcherine, Enzian) in *Gravity's Rainbow*. Pynchon is able to undermine Oedipa's authority, but he may have found such a "readerly" format constricting. It is interesting that *Gravity's Rainbow* borrows and builds on techniques established in *V.*, but owes very little to *Lot 49*.

3. See his illuminating study of the mystery story with a hole in it—or "whodonut," "Literature High and Low," in *The Fate of Reading and Other Essays*, p. 211.

4. Frank Kermode discusses this problem, essentially the question of giving meaningful form to statements about meaninglessness, in the context of Sartre's *Nausea*. See *The Sense of an Ending: Studies in the Theory of Fiction*, pp. 133–52.

5. Alexander Pope, *Essay on Man*, epistle 1, line 292.

6. *The Floating Opera*, p. 270.

7. That is, the two "solutions" most frequently proposed to what philosophy calls the Problem of Evil do not compel assent even on a fictional level.

8. *Structuralist Poetics: Structuralism, Linguistics, and the Study of Literature*, p. 193.

9. Sartre summarizes, "The world is mine because it is haunted by possibles, and the consciousness of each of these is a possible self-consciousness which I *am*; it is these possibles as such which give the world its unity and its meaning as the world" (*Being and Nothingness*, p. 158).

10. This point was brought home in Francis Ford Coppola's film *Apocalypse Now*, when Coppola unwisely decided to *show* what Kurtz meant by "the horror."

11. *Heart of Darkness*, p. 68.

12. David Cowart has pointed out that the painting described in this passage is the central panel of a real triptych owned by an anonymous buyer who, Cowart surmises, may be Pynchon himself. See his *Thomas Pynchon: The Art of Allusion*, pp. 24–30.

13. For discussions of Pynchon's metaphors from information theory, see especially Anne Mangel, "Maxwell's Demon, Entropy, Information: *The Crying of Lot 49*," in *Mindful Pleasures: Essays on Thomas Pynchon*, pp. 87–100; Peter L. Abernathy, "Entropy in Pynchon's *The Crying of Lot 49*"; Thomas H. Schaub, "*The Crying of Lot 49*: 'A Gentle Chill, an Ambiguity,'" in *Pynchon: The Voice of Ambiguity*, pp. 21–42.

14. Pynchon returns to this image in *Gravity's Rainbow*, where he makes all humanity a community of failed suicides. See chapter 4 below for a fuller discussion.

15. The rationalist philosopher Gottfried Wilhelm Leibniz (1646–1716) denied that there can be any interaction between thinking substances, such

as the human mind, and extended substances, such as the human body. Human beings, which he termed *monads*, were mind-body units; but mind could not affect body (as in willed action), and body could not affect mind (as in perception: as Leibniz put it, "the monads have no windows"). The *effect* of mind-body interaction was produced, he theorized, by the fact that God had willed all actions from eternity; consequently, for example, a volition and an action would occur simultaneously, but the volition could not actually produce the action. Oedipa's reasoning among the deaf-mutes seems similarly circuitous: are deaf-mutes similarly "windowless"?

Chapter Four

1. Simmon, "*Gravity's Rainbow* Described," p. 64.

2. Speer Morgan, "*Gravity's Rainbow*: What's the Big Idea?" The Big Idea is that entropy governs human life; Morgan disagrees.

3. Swigger, "Fictional Encyclopedism and the Cognitive Value of Literature," p. 351. For *Gravity's Rainbow* as an encyclopedic narrative, see especially Edward Mendelson, "Gravity's Encyclopedia," in Levine and Leverenz, eds., *Mindful Pleasures: Essays on Thomas Pynchon*. Most recently, Khachig Tololyan has assembled and correlated an enormous quantity of factual evidence (including several probable sources for details in *Gravity's Rainbow*) pertaining to the development of V-weapons; British and American responses to the V-2 during and after the war; the development of IG Farben and international cartels generally, from the Industrial Revolution to the present; psychological warfare during the war; and the continuity of war under the guise of peace, in "War as Background in *Gravity's Rainbow*," in Charles Clerc, ed., *Approaches to "Gravity's Rainbow."* This important study supplements Steven Weisenburger's groundbreaking article, "The End of History? Thomas Pynchon and the Uses of the Past," in *Twentieth Century Literature*.

4. The rocket's trajectory is identified with fate several times in the novel. The constellation of images that Pynchon draws on here—rocket, flight, fate, parabola, rainbow—seems to constitute a fairly widespread postwar *topos*. The Soviet poet Andrei Voznesensky, for instance, begins his "Ballad of the Parabola,"

Fate flies
     like a rocket, on a parabolic curve—
Mostly in darkness, but sometimes—
                it's a rainbow.

(*Selected Poems of Andrei Voznesensky*, p. 36). Pynchon's Peenemünde technicians use the same associations in a rocket-*koan*: "—What is it that flies? —Los!" (p. 454).

5. Hendin, "What is Thomas Pynchon Telling Us?" p. 90.

6. There are several excellent studies of Calvinism in *Gravity's Rainbow*.

See especially Scott Sanders, "Pynchon's Paranoid History"; John M. Krafft, " 'And How Far-Fallen,': Puritan Themes in *Gravity's Rainbow*"; Marcus Smith and Khachig Tölölyan, "The New Jeremiad: *Gravity's Rainbow*," in Richard Pearce, ed., *Critical Essays on Thomas Pynchon*. Joseph Slade takes an apparently opposite view, in which it is secularization that has deprived humanity of its ability to "read the primary text of Creation," but he identifies the sacred with the contradictory and the paradoxical, and thus regards Christian theology as a "rationalization" of the primitive acceptance of the unknown, perhaps best exemplified by the Herero religion. See his recent essays "Thomas Pynchon, Postindustrial Humanist," *Technology and Culture*, and "Religion, Psychology, Sex, and Love in *Gravity's Rainbow*," in Charles Clerc, ed., *Approaches to "Gravity's Rainbow."*

7. Thorburn, "A Dissent on Pynchon."

8. Josiah E. Dubois, who was head of the prosecution in the 1947 Nuremberg trial of Farben's board of directors, has written an account of his investigations that emphasizes the evidence for the charge (dismissed by the tribunal) that the Farben executives actively promoted the war. See DuBois and Edward Johnson, *The Devil's Chemists: 24 Conspirators of the International Farben Cartel Who Manufacture Wars*. A more recent exposé, Joseph Borkin's *The Crime and Punishment of I. G. Farben*, brings in more evidence substantiating DuBois's contentions.

9. See Jacob Bronowski, *The Common Sense of Science*, p. 64.

10. James Collins, *A History of Modern European Philosophy*, p. 96.

11. See Harold F. Blum, *Time's Arrow and Evolution*.

12. Walter Dornberger, who was head of the entire German rocket development program, provides a great deal of technical evidence for this thesis in his book *V-2*. Sir Philip Joubert de la Fierté, air chief marshall of Great Britain during World War II, describes the effect of the V-weapons on England and concludes, "V1 and V2 in action in 1940, even in 1943, would have been decisive weapons" (*Rocket*, p. 120).

13. Olderman, "Thomas Pynchon."

14. See Wernher von Braun and Frederick I. Ordway III, *History of Rocketry and Space Travel*, p. 100.

15. In this and numerous other respects, *Gravity's Rainbow* is close to the radical psychohistory of Norman O. Brown in *Life Against Death: The Psychoanalytical Meaning of History*. For a study of Brown's influence on Pynchon, see Lawrence Wolfley, "Repression's Rainbow: The Presence of Norman O. Brown in Pynchon's Big Novel."

16. Joel D. Black traces a number of these associations to an antimechanistic strain in Anglo-American and German romanticism. See his important study "Probing a Post-Romantic Paleontology: Thomas Pynchon's *Gravity's Rainbow*."

17. Bronowski, *The Common Sense of Science*, pp. 64–65.

18. He loses what Kurt Mondaugen calls "temporal bandwidth...the width of your present, your *now*" (p. 509). But Mondaugen is a Nazi collaborator, and in exalting temporal bandwidth, which is really the capacity of containing history, he may be upholding Their idea of historical totality. Other passages suggest that the inability to make sense of your Now may be the inability to comprehend Official History—which may have its positive aspects. Later in the novel, some of Slothrop's doper companions have trouble understanding the Nuremberg Trials: "No one Slothrop has listened to is clear who's trying whom for what, but remember that these are mostly brains ravaged by antisocial and mindless pleasures" (p. 681). In the context of a conspiracy between corporations throughout the war, these trials were a travesty: they vindicated the Farben executives of charges of fomenting war and collaborating in the death camps, among other things (see note 8 above). A certain lack of clarity about "who's trying whom for what" seems warranted. And Pynchon suggests throughout the novel that "brains ravaged by antisocial and mindless pleasures" have a desirable perspective. In fact, "Mindless Pleasures" was the original title of *Gravity's Rainbow*.

19. Herbert Marcuse, *One-Dimensional Man: Studies in the Ideology of Advanced Industrial Society*. James I. McClintock notes Marcuse's influence on *Gravity's Rainbow* in "United States Revisited: Pynchon and Zamiatin," p. 481. In his study responding to, and building on, Marcuse's work, *Many Dimensional Man: Decentralizing Self, Society, and the Sacred*, David Ogilvy argues for a decentralized psychology that might take Slothrop as an ideal: "Contrary to currently debased rhetoric about authenticity and identity crises, the least free persons are those whose personality is single to the point of predictability. The model of many dimensional man is therefore a model of multiple selves within each person. Each self is a source of differing interpretations of those interactions through which a single person carries its several selves" (p. 59). Sanford S. Ames, in a brilliant if highly condensed article, "Pynchon and Visible Language: Ecriture," finds a useful gloss in Gilles Deleuze and Felix Guattari's *Anti-Oedipus*, and suggests that Pynchon is dealing with the individual's obsessive need for self-consolidation.

20. The other major instance of a father sacrificing his son in *Gravity's Rainbow* is Broderick Slothrop's sale of Infant Tyrone to Dr. Jamf. Significantly, the elder Slothrop offers up his child to the twentieth century's twin gods of science and industry. Both Gottfried and Slothrop resemble Isaac, the prototype of the sacrificial offering in the closing sections, but they also resemble the "only-begotten son" whom God the Father killed in the central episode of the Christian myth. In *Gravity's Rainbow* the providential parabola stands for a patriarchal system that expresses its true values in filicide and aims to destroy all future generations.

21. For intelligent and intelligible discussions of this theorem, see J. Van Heijenoort, "Gödel's Theorem"; and Ernest Naegel and John R. Newman, *Gödel's Proof*.

22. The move away from attempts to construct a comprehensive explanatory system has been striking in twentieth-century science. See especially Werner Heisenberg, "'Closed Theory' in Modern Science," *Across the Frontiers*, pp. 39–46; and Nicholas Capaldi, *Philosophy of Science: The Historical Development of Scientific Concepts and Their Philosophical Implications.*

23. For an excellent discussion of the personal and political dimensions of such betrayal, see John M. Krafft, "Anarcho-Romanticism and the Metaphysics of Counterforce: Alex Comfort and Thomas Pynchon."

24. Morrison, rpt. in Mendelson, ed., *Pynchon: A Collection of Critical Essays*, p. 192.

25. Again, the Hereros are closer to the Jews than to Christians; the feast of Passover also celebrates deliverance, notably from God's wrath against the firstborn of Egypt.

26. "Newsmakers," *Newsweek*, 20 May 1974.

27. Frank Kermode, *The Sense of an Ending: Studies in the Theory of Fiction*, p. 7.

28. Dornberger, *V-2*, p. 111.

29. The reference is to Reed's 1972 novel *Mumbo Jumbo*, which also amasses "period" detail and documentation to bolster its account of a Masonic conspiracy to stifle a Black uprising called "Jez Grew."

30. This is one of many instances in which Pynchon invokes film techniques (others are the fade, the dissolve, the wipe, the focus, the zoom, and the reverse zoom) to provide a partial context for textual innovations. Some of the best criticism of *Gravity's Rainbow* deals with filmic aspects of the novel. See especially David Cowart, "Cinematic Auguries of the Third Reich in *Gravity's Rainbow*"; Bernard F. Dick, "At the Crossroads of Time: Types of Simultaneity in Literature and Film"; Scott Simmon, "Beyond the Theatre of War: *Gravity's Rainbow* as Film"; Charles Clerc, "Film in *Gravity's Rainbow*," in Charles Clerc, ed., *Approaches to "Gravity's Rainbow."*

31. Many sections follow idiosyncratic standards of internal coherence. The previously mentioned episode framed by the movie camera, for instance, insists on its own self-perpetuation. The Kenosha Kid passage, also in book one, is another such aesthetic unit: it achieves completion through a device of attaching multiple explicit meanings to an apparently nonsense phrase, and in this paradoxical way frames Slothrop's drug-conditioned night journey with its insistence on a plurality of possible interpretations. Such sections (and there are many more of them) are almost set pieces. They are complete in themselves; they can be appreciated apart from their situation in the novel; yet they gain significance and complexity by being woven into the context with threads of allusion, imagery, and thematic concern.

32. Kermode, *Sense of an Ending*, p. 138.

33. The Rocket is also associated with the "Church of Rome" in this

passage, another reminder that the theory of a preexisting historical trajectory is theological in origin.

34. The narrator does occasionally employ the future tense, often in contexts where prophecy is especially disconcerting: during the love scene with Bianca, the narrator reports of Slothrop, "Sure he'll stay for a while, but eventually he'll go, and for this he is to be counted, after all, among the Zone's lost" (p. 470). But repeated use of the future tense undermines the authority of such statements; a few pages later, "Slothrop will think he sees her . . . he will see her lose her footing . . . he will lunge after her without thinking much, slip himself . . . and be flipped that easy over the side . . . " (p. 491). The eerily prophetic tone diminishes as the passage turns into a straightforward transition, using future constructions to express present action. It is worth noting in addition that the narrator is sometimes unsure about what *has* happened. The long initial conversation between Tchitcherine and Wimpe, for instance, is couched in terms of hypothesis: "Certainly he *could* have known Wimpe" (p. 344). "What did Tchitcherine have to say? Was Tchitcherine there at all?" (p. 345). Omniscience appears to be an unstable quality in *Gravity's Rainbow*.

35. This convention may be even more important than the film convention in *Gravity's Rainbow*. It supplements or replaces film notations at many points, providing an additional context for bizarre turns in the narrative. When the discussion of Pirate Prentice's odd occupation early in the book is suddenly transposed to a music hall stage, for instance (pp. 12–13), the hallucinatory quality suggests that the "theatre" or controlling consciousness of the passage is the domain of characters such as the dope-crazed moviemaker Gerhardt von Göll, the dealer Saüre Bummer (whose name, translated as "acid bummer" or Anglicized as "sorry bummer," suggests the quintessential bad trip), or any of their numerous friends who subscribe to a heretical reading of Their motto, "Better living through chemistry." Allusions to the drug experience help license the narrator's rapid shifts in perspective, his exaggerated attentiveness, and his seizures of paranoia; furthermore, they provide a sort of ludic rationale for the sensibility that devotes almost two pages to setting up lines like Bloody Chiclitz's "For DeMille, young fur-henchmen can't be rowing" (p. 559). The passage noting effects of the drug Oneirine (from the Greek *oneiros*, "dream") describes many characteristics of the novel itself (pp. 702–03). For a related discussion, see Raymond M. Olderman, "The New Consciousness and the Old System," in Charles Clerc, ed., *Approaches to "Gravity's Rainbow."*

36. Hugh Kenner, *Joyce's Voices*, p. 18.

37. For Rilke this total surrender is a precondition for recognizing the seamless continuity between life and death, self and world. In the last stanza of his Tenth Elegy, Blicero's favorite poem, he celebrates the cataclysmic inversion of values that turns self-abnegation and even death into triumph. The imagery transposes easily into the context of rocket-metaphysics:

And we, who have always thought
of happiness climbing, would feel
the emotion that almost startles
when happiness falls.

(*Duino Elegies*, p. 85).

38. von Braun, *History of Rocketry and Space Travel*, p. 116. Dornberger provides a further interesting note. His own elite staff holed up near the foot of the Hartz Mountains, in a town called Bad Sachsa (*V-2*, p. 266). Pynchon performs miracles of displacement with this last name. He transfers the "Sachsa" part to a character, Leni's lover Peter Sachsa, but keeps the town, making it the scene of Greta Erdmann's infanticides and rechristening it, approximately, Bad Karma.

39. von Braun, *History of Rocketry*, p. 112.

40. In "Pynchon and Visible Language," Sanford S. Ames observes, "The real obscenities in *Gravity's Rainbow* are those visions of supreme value outside the text of life for which the rocket reaches and strains leaving in its wake evacuation, waste, and destruction, not only of landscape but the intimate territories of the embattled paranoid private citizen in his theatre of shadows" (p. 171).

41. Simmon, "*Gravity's Rainbow* Described," p. 64.

42. Olderman, "Thomas Pynchon," pp. 500–507.

Bibliography

Primary Sources

Pynchon, Thomas. *The Crying of Lot 49*. New York: Bantam, 1967.
_____. "Entropy." *Kenyon Review* 22 (1960): 277–92.
_____. *Gravity's Rainbow*. New York: Viking, 1973.
_____. "Low-Lands." *New World Writing* 16 (1960): 85–108.
_____. "Mortality and Mercy in Vienna." *Epoch* 9 (1959): 195–213.
_____. *V*. New York: Bantam, 1964.
_____. "Under the Rose." *Noble Savage* 3 (1961): 233–51.

Secondary Sources

Abernathy, Peter L. "Entropy in Pynchon's *The Crying of Lot 49*." *Critique* 14, no. 2 (1972): 18–33.
Adams, Henry. *The Education of Henry Adams*. Ed. Ernest Samuels. 1918; rpt. Boston: Houghton Mifflin, 1973.
Alter, Robert. "The Self-Conscious Moment: Reflections on the Aftermath of Modernism." *TriQuarterly* 33 (Spring 1975): 209–30.
Altieri, Charles. "The Hermeneutics of Literary Interdeterminacy: A Dissent From the New Orthodoxy." *New Literary History* 10(1978): 71–99.
_____. "Presence and Reference in a Literary Text: The Example of Williams' 'This is Just to Say.'" *Critical Inquiry*, Spring 1979, pp. 489–510.
_____. "The Qualities of Action: A Theory of Middles in Literature." *Boundary-2* 5 (1977): 323–50, 899–917.
Ames, Sanford S. "Pynchon and Visible Language: Ecriture." *International Fiction Review* 4 (1977): 170–73.
Aquinas, St. Thomas. *Summa Theologica*. In *Thomas Aquinas*. Great Books of the Westeern World. Ed. Robert Maynard Hutchins. Chicago: Encyclopaedia Brittanica, 1952.
Aristotle. *The Poetics*. In *The Basic Works of Aristotle*. Ed. Richard B. McKeon. New York: Random House, 1971. Pp. 1454–87.

Barnett, Lincoln. *The Universe and Dr. Einstein.* Intro. Albert Einstein. New York: Bantam, 1968.

Barth, John. *The Floating Opera.* New York: Avon, 1956.

———. "The Literature of Exhaustion." *Atlantic*, August 1967, pp. 29–34.

Barthes, Roland. *Roland Barthes.* Trans. Richard Howard. New York: Hill and Wang, 1977.

———. *S/Z: An Essay.* Trans. Richard Miller. New York: Hill and Wang, 1974.

Black, Joel D. "Probing a Post-Romantic Paleontology: Thomas Pynchon's *Gravity's Rainbow.*" *Boundary-2* 8 (1980): 229–54.

Bloom, Harold, et al. *Deconstruction and Criticism.* New York: Seabury Press, 1979.

Blum, Harold F. *Time's Arrow and Evolution.* New York: Harper Torchbooks, 1962.

Bogel, Fredric V. "Fables of Knowing: Melodrama and Related Forms." *Genre*, Spring 1978, pp. 83–108.

Bohm, David. *Causality and Chance in Modern Physics.* Philadelphia: University of Pennsylvania Press, 1957.

Borkin, Joseph. *The Crime and Punishment of I. G. Farben.* New York: Free Press, 1978.

Bronowski, Jacob. *The Common Sense of Science.* Cambridge, Mass.: Harvard University Press, 1978.

Brown, Norman O. *Life Against Death: The Psychoanalytical Meaning of History.* Middletown, Conn.: Wesleyan University Press, 1959.

Burtt, E. A. *The Metaphysical Foundations of Modern Science.* New York: Anchor, 1954.

Calhoun, John C. "The Concept of Revolution and Its Influence on the Genesis of Art in the Work of Thomas Pynchon." *Perspectives on Contemporary Literature* 2 (1976): 40–52.

Capaldi, Nicholas. *Philosophy of Science: The Historical Development of Scientific Concepts and Their Philosophical Implications.* New York: Monarch Press, 1966.

Čapek, Milič. *The Philosophical Impact of Contemporary Physics.* New York: Van Nostrand, 1961.

Clerc, Charles, ed. *Approaches to "Gravity's Rainbow."* Columbus, Ohio: Ohio State University Press, 1982.

Coleman, James A. *Relativity for the Layman.* New York: Signet, 1954.

Collins, James. *A History of Modern European Philosophy.* Milwaukee: Bruce Publishing Co., 1954.

Conrad, Joseph. *Heart of Darkness.* New York: Signet, 1950.

Cowart, David. "Cinematic Auguries of the Third Reich in *Gravity's Rainbow.*" *Literature/Film Quarterly* 6 (1978): 364–70.

———. "Pynchon's *The Crying of Lot 49* and the Paintings of Remedios Varo." *Critique* 18, no. 3 (1977): 19–26.

———. *Thomas Pynchon: The Art of Allusion.* Carbondale: Southern Illinois University Press, 1980.

Culler, Jonathan. *Structuralist Poetics: Structuralism, Linguistics, and the Study of Literature.* Ithaca, N.Y.: Cornell University Press, 1975.

Davis, Robert Murray. "Parody, Paranoia, and the Dead End of Language in *The Crying of Lot 49.*" *Genre* 5 (1972): 367–77.

Derrida, Jacques. *Speech and Phenomena, and Other Essays on Husserl's Theory of Signs.* Trans. David B. Allison. Evanston, Ill.: Northwestern University Press, 1973.

Dick, Bernard F. "At the Crossroads of Time: Types of Simultaneity in Literature and Film." *George Review* 33, no. 1 (1979): 423–32.

Dickstein, Morris. "Black Humor and History: Fiction in the Sixties." *Partisan Review* 43, no. 2 (1976): 185–211.

Dornberger, Walter. *V-2.* Trans. James Clough and Geoffrey Halliday. New York: Viking Press, 1958.

Dubois, Josiah E., in collaboration with Edward Johnson. *The Devil's Chemists: 24 Conspirators of the International Farben Cartel Who Manufacture Wars.* Boston: Beacon Press, 1957.

Fahy, Joseph. "Thomas Pynchon's *V.* and Mythology." *Critique* 18, no. 3. (1977): 5–17.

Foucault, Michel. *The Order of Things: An Archaeology of the Human Sciences.* New York: Vintage, 1973.

Gillespie, Charles Coulston. *The Edge of Objectivity: An Essay in the History of Scientific Ideas.* Princeton, N.J.: Princeton University Press, 1960.

Gödel, Kurt. "Some Metamathematical Results on Completeness and Consistency, on Formally Undecidable Propositions of *Principia mathematica* and Related Systems I," and "On Completeness and Consistency." In *Frege and Gödel: Two Fundamental Texts in Mathematical Logic*, pp. 83–108. Ed. Jean van Heijenoort. London: Oxford University Press, 1970.

Golden, Robert E. "Mass Man and Modernism: Violence in Pynchon's *V.*" *Critique* 14, no. 2 (1972): 5–17.

Graff, Gerald. "Babbitt at the Abyss: The Social Context of Postmodern American Fiction." *TriQuarterly* 33 (Spring 1975): 305–37.

Greenberg, Alvin. "The Underground Woman: An Excursion into the V-ness of Thomas Pynchon." *Chelsea* 27 (1969): 58–65.

Hall, James. "The New Pleasures of the Imagination." *Virginia Quarterly Review* 46 (1970): 596–612.

Hartman, Geoffrey H. *The Fate of Reading and Other Essays.* Chicago: University of Chicago Press, 1975.

Hassan, Ihab. *The Dismemberment of Orpheus*. New York: Oxford University Press, 1971.

_____. "The Dismemberment of Orpheus: Notes on Form and Antiform in Contemporary Literature." In *Learners and Discerners: A Newer Criticism*, pp. 135–65. Ed. Robert Scholes. Charlottesville: University Press of Virginia, 1964.

Heijenoort, J. Van. "Gödel's Theorem." *Encyclopedia of Philosophy*. Vols. 3 and 4, pp. 348–57. New York: MacMillan, 1967.

Heisenberg, Werner. "'Closed Theory' in Modern Science." In *Across the Frontiers*, pp. 39–46. Trans. Peter Heath. New York: Harper and Row, 1974.

Hendin, Josephine. "What is Thomas Pynchon Telling Us?" *Harper's* 250 (1975): 89–92.

_____. *Vulnerable People: A View of American Fiction since 1945*. New York: Oxford University Press, 1978.

Holquist, Michael, and Walter Reed. "Six Theses on the Novel—and Some Metaphors." *New Literary History* 11 (1980): 413–33.

Hunt, John W. "Comic Escape and Anti-Vision: The Novels of Joseph Heller and Thomas Pynchon." In *Adversity and Grace: Studies in Recent American Literature*, pp. 87–112. Ed. Nathan A. Scott, Jr. Chicago: University of Chicago Press, 1968.

Hyman, Stanley Edgar. "The Goddess and the Schlemihl (Thomas Pynchon)." In *Standards: A Chronicle of Books for Our Time*, pp. 138–42. New York: Horizon, 1966.

Joubert de la Fierté, Sir Philip. *Rocket*. London: Hutchinson and Co., 1957.

Kant, Immanuel. *The Critique of Pure Reason*. Trans. Norman Kemp Smith. New York: St. Martin's, 1965.

Kappel, Lawrence. "Psychic Geography in *Gravity's Rainbow*." *Contemporary Literature* 21, no. 2 (1980): 225–51.

Kazin, Alfred. "Absurdity as a Contemporary State: Ellison to Pynchon." In *Bright Book of Life: American Novelists and Storytellers from Hemingway to Mailer*, pp. 243–81. Boston: Little, Brown, and Co., 1973.

Kenner, Hugh. "Art in a Closed Field." In *Learners and Discerners: A Newer Criticism*, pp. 109–33. Ed. Robert Scholes. Charlottesville: University Press of Virginia, 1964.

_____. *Flaubert, Joyce, and Beckett: The Stoic Comedians*. Boston: Beacon Press, 1962.

_____. *Joyce's Voices*. Berkeley: University of California Press, 1978.

Kermode, Frank. *The Sense of an Ending: Studies in the Theory of Fiction*. New York: Oxford University Press, 1967.

_____. "Sensing Endings." *Nineteenth-Century Fiction* 33, no. 1 (1978): 144–55.

_____. "The Use of the Codes." In *Approaches to Poetics*, pp. 51–79. Ed. Seymour Chatman. New York: Columbia University Press, 1973.

Kierkegaard, Soren. *Fear and Trembling*. In *Selections from the Writings of Soren Kierkegaard*, pp. 119–52. New York: Anchor, 1960.

Krafft, John M. "Anarcho-Romanticism and the Metaphysics of Counterforce: Alex Comford and Thomas Pynchon." *Paunch* 40–41 (1975): 78–106.

_____. "'And How Far-Fallen': Puritan Themes in *Gravity's Rainbow*." *Critique* 18, no. 3 (1977): 55–73.

Larner, Jeremy. "The New Schlemihl." *Partisan Review* 30 (1963): 273–76.

Lehan, Richard. "Man and His Fictions: Ellison, Pynchon, Heller, and Barth." In *A Dangerous Crossing: French Literary Existentialism and the Modern American Novel*, pp. 157–62. Carbondale: Southern Illinois University Press, 1973.

Leland, John P. "Pynchon's Linguistic Demon: *The Crying of Lot 49*." *Critique* 16, no. 2 (1974): 45–53.

Lentricchia, Frank. *The Gaiety of Language: An Essay on the Radical Poetics of W. B. Yeats and Wallace Stevens*. Berkeley: University of California Press, 1968.

Levine, George, and David Leverenz, eds. *Mindful Pleasures: Essays on Thomas Pynchon*. Boston: Little, Brown, and Co., 1976.

Levine, George. "V-2." *Partisan Review* 40 (1973): 517–29.

Lewis, R. W. B. "Days of Wrath and Laughter." In *Trials of the Word*, pp. 228–43. New Haven, Conn.: Yale University Press, 1965.

Lhamon, W. T., Jr. "Break and Enter to Breakaway: Scotching Modernism in the Social Novel of the American Sixties." *Boundary-2* 3 (1975): 289–306.

_____. "The Most Irresponsible Bastard." *New Republic*, 168 (1973): 24–28.

_____. "Pentecost, Promiscuity, and Pynchon's *V*.: From the Scaffold to the Impulsive." *Twentieth Century Literature* 21, no. 2 (1975): 163–75.

Locke, Richard. "*Gravity's Rainbow*, by Thomas Pynchon." *New York Times Book Review*, 11 March 1973, pp. 1–3, 12, 14.

Lodge, David. *The Modes of Modern Writing: Metaphor, Metonymy, and the Typology of Modern Literature*. Ithaca, N.Y.: Cornell University Press, 1977.

MacAdam, Alfred. "Pynchon as Satirist: To Write, to Mean." *Yale Review* 67 (1975): 555–66.

Mackey, Louis. "Paranoia, Pynchon, and Preterition." *Sub-Stance* 30 (1981): 16–30.

McClintock, James I. "United States Revisited: Pynchon and Zamiatin." *Contemporary Literature* 18, no. 4 (1980): 475–90.

McConnell, Frank. "The Corpse of the Dragon: Notes on Postromantic Fiction." *TriQuarterly* 33 (1975): 273–303.

_____. *Four Postwar American Novelists: Bellow, Mailer, Barth, Pynchon.* Chicago: University of Chicago Press, 1977.

McHale, Brian. "Modernist Reading, Postmodern Text: The Case of *Gravity's Rainbow.*" *Poetics Today* 1, nos. 1–2 (1979): 86–110.

Marcuse, Herbert. *One-Dimensional Man: Studies in the Ideology of Advanced Industrial Society.* Boston: Beacon Press, 1964.

Marx, Leo. *The Machine in the Garden: Technology and the Pastoral Ideal in America.* New York: Oxford University Press, 1964.

Mendelson, Edward, ed. *Pynchon: A Collection of Critical Essays.* Englewood Cliffs, N.J.: Prentice-Hall, 1978.

_____. "Pynchon's Gravity." *Yale Review* 62 (1973): 624–31.

Morgan, Speer. "*Gravity's Rainbow*: What's the Big Idea?" *Modern Fiction Studies* 23 (1977): 199–216.

Morris, Robert K. "Jumping Off the Golden Gate Bridge." *Nation* 217 (1973): 53–54.

Musil, Robert. *The Man without Qualities.* Trans. Eithne Wilkins and Ernst Kaiser. New York: Coward-McCann, 1954.

Muste, John M. "The Mandala in *Gravity's Rainbow.*" *Boundary-2* 9, no. 2 (1981): 163–79.

Nadeau, Robert. *Readings from the New Book on Nature: Physics and Metaphysics in the Modern Novel.* Amherst: University of Massachusetts Press, 1981.

Naegel, Ernest, and John R. Newman. *Gödel's Proof.* New York: New York University Press, 1958.

New, Melvyn. "Profaned and Stenciled Texts: In Search of Pynchon's *V.*" *Georgia Review* 33, no. 1 (1979): 395–412.

Newton, Isaac. *Mathematical Principles of Natural Philosophy and System of the World.* Trans. Andrew Motte, Ed. Floria Cajori. Berkeley: University of California Press, 1934.

Ogilvy, James. *Many Dimensional Man: Decentralizing Self, Society, and the Sacred.* New York: Oxford University Press, 1977.

Olderman, Raymond M. "Thomas Pynchon." *Contemporary Literature* 20 (1979): 500–507.

_____. "The Illusion and Possibility of Conspiracy: Thomas Pynchon, *V.*, and *The Crying of Lot 49.*" In *Beyond the Waste Land: A Study of the American Novel in the Nineteen-Sixties*, pp. 123–49. New Haven, Conn.: Yale University Press, 1972.

Ozier, Lance W. "Antipointsman/AntiMexico: Some Mathematical Imagery in *Gravity's Rainbow.*" *Critique* 16, no. 2 (1974): 73–90.

_____. "The Calculus of Transformation: More Mathematical Imagery in

Gravity's Rainbow.'' Twentieth Century Literature 21, no. 2 (1975): 193–210.

Paley, William. *Natural Theology: Selections.* Ed. Frederick Ferré. Indianapolis: Bobbs-Merrill, 1963.

Pavlov, I. P. *Conditioned Reflexes: An Investigation of the Cerebral Cortext.* Trans. G. V. Anrep. 1927; rpt. New York: Dover, 1960.

Patteson, Richard. "What Stencil Knew: Structure and Certainty in Pynchon's *V.'' Critique* 16, no. 2 (1974): 30–44.

Pearce, Richard, Ed. *Critical Essays on Thomas Pynchon.* Boston: G. K. Hall, 1981.

Plater, William M. *The Grim Phoenix: Reconstructing Thomas Pynchon.* Bloomington: Indiana University Press, 1978.

Plimpton, George. "Mata Hari With a Clockwork Eye, Alligators in the Sewer.'' *New York Times Book Review,* 21 April 1963, p. 5.

Poirier, Richard. "The Importance of Thomas Pynchon.'' *Twentieth Century Literature* 21, no. 2 (1975): 151–62.

———. "Rocket Power.'' *Saturday Review of the Arts* 1, no. 3 (1973): 59–64.

Pope, Alexander. *An Essay on Man.* In *The Poems of Alexander Pope.* Ed. John Butt. New Haven, Conn.: Yale University Press, 1963.

Price, Martin. "The Fictional Contract.'' In *Literary Theory and Structure: Essays in Honor of William K. Wimsatt,* pp. 151–78. Ed. Frank Brady, John Palmer, and Martin Price. New Haven, Conn.: Yale University Press, 1973.

Pütz, Manfred. *The Story of Identity: American Fiction of the Sixties.* Stuttgard: Metzlersche Verlagsbuchhandlung, 1979.

Pynchon, William. *The Diary of William Pynchon of Salem.* Ed. Fitch Edward Oliver. Boston: Houghton Mifflin and Co., 1890.

Reck-Malleczewan, Friedrich Percyval. *Diary of a Man in Despair.* Trans. Paul Rubens. New York: Collier Books, 1970.

Richter, David H. *Fable's End: Completeness and Closure in Rhetorical Fiction.* Chicago: University of Chicago Press, 1974.

Reed, Ishmael. *Mumbo Jumbo.* New York: Avon, 1972.

Rilke, Rainier Maria. *Duino Elegies.* Trans. J. B. Leishman and Stephen Spender. New York: Norton Library, 1939.

Rother, James. "Parafiction: The Adjacent Universes of Barth, Barthelme, Pynchon, and Nabokov.'' *Boundary-2* 5, no. 1 (1976): 21–43.

Runes, Dagobert D., ed. *A Dictionary of Philosophy.* New York: Philosophical Library, 1960.

Safer, Elaine B. "The Allusive Mode and Black Humor in Barth's *Giles Goat-Boy* and Pynchon's *Gravity's Rainbow.'' Renascence* 32, no. 2 (1980): 89–104.

Said, Edward W. *Beginnings: Intention and Method.* New York: Basic Books, 1975.

———. "Contemporary Fiction and Criticism." *Tri-Quarterly* 33 (1975): 231–56.

Sanders, Scott. "Pynchon's Paranoid History." *Twentieth Century Literature* 21, no. 2 (1975): 177–92.

Sartre, Jean-Paul. *Being and Nothingness.* Trans. Hazel E. Barnes. New York: Washington Square Press, 1971.

Schaub, Thomas Hill. "Open Letter in Response to Edward Mendelson's 'The Sacred, the Profane, and *The Crying of Lot 49.*'" *Boundary-2* 5 (1976): 93–101.

Schaub, Thomas H. *Pynchon: The Voice of Ambiguity.* Urbana: University of Illinois Press, 1981.

Schmitz, Neil. "Describing the Demon: The Appeal of Thomas Pynchon." *Partisan Review* 42 (1975): 112–25.

Scholes, Robert. *Fabulation and Metafiction.* Urbana: University of Illinois Press, 1979.

———. "Mithridates, he died old." In *The Sounder Few: Essays from "The Hollins Critic,"* pp. 173–91. Ed. R. H. W. Dillard, George Garreet, and John Rees Moore. Athens: University of Georgia Press, 1971.

Schultz, Max F. "The Politics of Parody and the Comic Apocalypses of Jorge Luis Borges, Thomas Berger, Thomas Pynchon, and Robert Coover." In *Black Humor Fiction of the Sixties: A Pluralistic Definition of Man and His World*, pp. 77–90. Athens: Ohio University Press, 1973.

Seed, David. "The Fictional Labyrinths of Thomas Pynchon." *Critical Quarterly* 18 (1976): 73–81.

Siegel, Mark R. "Creative Paranoia: Understanding the System of *Gravity's Rainbow.*" *Critique* 18, no. 3 (1977): 39–54.

———. *Pynchon: Creative Paranoia in "Gravity's Rainbow."* Port Washington, N.Y.: Kennikat Press, 1978.

Simmon, Scott. "Beyond the Theater of War: *Gravity's Rainbow* as Film." *Literature/Film Quarterly* 6 (1978): 347–63.

———. "A Character Index: *Gravity's Rainbow.*" *Critique* 16, no. 2 (1974): 68–72.

———. "*Gravity's Rainbow* Described." *Critique* 16, no. 2 (1974): 54–67.

Slade, Joseph W. "Escaping Rationalization: Options for the Self in *Gravity's Rainbow.*" *Critique* 18, no. 3 (1977): 27–38.

———. *Thomas Pynchon.* New York: Warner Paperback, 1974.

———. "Thomas Pynchon, Postindustrial Humanist." *Technology and Culture* 23 (1982): 53–72.

Smith, Marcus, and Khachig Tölölyan. "The New Jeremiad: *Gravity's*

Rainbow." In *Critical Essays on Thomas Pynchon*, pp. 169–86. Ed. Richard Pearce. Boston: G. K. Hall, 1981.

Swigger, Ronald T. "Fictional Encyclopedism and the Cognitive Value of Literature." *Comparative Literature Studies* 12 (1975): 351–66.

Stevens, Wallace. *Ideas of Order.* New York: Alfred A. Knopf, 1936.

Tanner, Tony. "The American Novelist as Entropologist." *London Magazine* 10, no. 7 (1970): 5–18.

_____. *City of Words: American Fiction, 1950–1970.* London: Jonathan Cape, 1971.

_____. *Thomas Pynchon.* New York: Methuen, 1982.

Thorburn, David. "A Dissent on Pynchon." *Commentary* 56 (1973): 68–70.

Tölölyan, Khachig. "Criticism as Symptom: Thomas Pynchon and the Crisis of the Humanities." *New Orleans Review* 5 (1977): 314–18.

_____. "The Fishy Poisson: Allusions to Statistics in *Gravity's Rainbow.*" *Notes on Modern American Literature* 4 (1979).

Vacha, J. E. "It Could Happen Here: The Rise of the Political Scenario Novel." *American Quarterly* 29 (1977): 194–206.

Vesterman, William. "Pynchon's Poetry." *Twentieth Century Literature* 21, no. 2. (1975): 211–20.

von Braun, Wernher, and Frederick I. Ordway III. *History of Rocketry and Space Travel.* 3d ed. New York: Thomas Y. Cromwell Co., 1975.

Voznesensky, Andrei. *Selected Poems of Andrei Voznesensky.* Trans. Anselm Hollo. New York: Grove Press, 1964.

Wagner, Richard. *Tannhäuser.* In *The Authentic Librettos of the Wagner Operas.* New York: Crown Publishers, 1938.

Weisenburger, Steven C. "Accelerated Grimace: American Fiction in the Age of Speed." Ph.D. diss. University of Washington, 1978.

_____. "The End of History? Thomas Pynchon and the Uses of the Past." *Twentieth Century Literature* 25, no. 1 (1979): 54–72.

_____. "Thomas Pynchon, Gödel's Theorem, the Rhetoric of Mathematics." Unpublished paper, 1977.

Welsh, Alexander. "Realism as a Practical and Cosmic Joke." *Novel,* Fall 1975, pp. 23–39.

Wiener, Norbert. *The Human Use of Human Beings: Cybernetics and Society.* New York: Avon, 1954.

Wittgenstein, Ludwig. *Notebooks: 1914–1916.* Trans. G. E. M. Anscombe. New York: Harper Torchbooks, 1961.

_____. *Philosophical Investigations.* Trans. G. E. M. Anscombe. New York: MacMillan, 1958.

_____. *Tractatus Logico-Philosophicus.* Trans. D. F. Pears and B. F. McGuinness. London: Routledge and Kegan Paul, 1974.

Wolfley, Lawrence C. "Repression's Rainbow: The Presence of Norman O. Brown in Pynchon's Big Novel." *PMLA* 92 (1978): 873–79.

Wood, Michael. "Rocketing to the Apocalypse." *New York Review of Books* 20 (1973): 22–23.

Young, James Dean. "The Enigma Variations of Thomas Pynchon." *Critique* 10, no. 1 (1967): 69–77.

Zavarzadeh, Mas'ud. *The Mythopoeic Reality: The Postwar American Nonfiction Novel*. Urbana: University of Illinois Press, 1977.

Index